Popular Complete Smart Series

Complete ScienceSmart®

Grade 4

Monica Whatley

Credits

Photos (Front Cover "satellite dish" David Hughes/123RF.com, "gears" alex_star/123RF.com, "jet plane" Lars Christenen/123RF.com. Back Cover "girl on left"/123RF.com, "boy" Jose Manuel Gelpi Diaz/123RF.com, "girl in middle"/123RF.com, "girl on right" Paul Hakimata/123RF.com, "memo board" Sandra Van Der Steen/123RF.com, "children"/123RF.com.)

Copyright © 2015 Popular Book Company (Canada) Limited

Printed in China

ISBN: 978-1-897457-76-4

Table of Contents

Section **1**

Understanding Life Systems

Students will understand that a habitat provides the organisms that live in it with their basic needs such as food and water. They will also investigate the different types of habitats and how some living things survive in their habitats with their unique features. Human interactions with habitats and the impacts of human activities on habitats will also be discussed. Additionally, students will learn about the food chain and classify animals into three groups based on their diets.

ISBN: 978-1-897457-76-4

Understanding Structures and Mechanisms

Students will review the use of the six simple machines. They will then study two special kinds of wheels: pulleys and gears, and learn how they transfer, transform, change the speed and direction of motion, and change the amount of force needed to move objects. They will also identify and observe everyday machines that use gears and pulleys and study the advantages they provide.

ISBN: 978-1-897457-76-4

Table of Contents

Understanding Matter and Energy

Students will study the properties of light and sound by investigating how they interact with various objects in the environment. They will discover that materials can be used to transmit, reflect, or absorb light and sound. The impact of technologies related to sound and light on our everyday lives, including their use of energy, will also be examined. Students will also learn that some protective equipment is necessary in protecting themselves from excess light or sound.

ISBN: 978-1-897457-76-4

Understanding Earth and Space Systems

Students will be introduced to the study of rocks and minerals. They will study the properties of rocks and minerals and examine the different types of rocks and minerals found on Earth. They will investigate the unique characteristics and properties of rocks and minerals and how rocks were formed. Students will also become aware that human uses of rocks and minerals not only alter landscapes, but also affect the environment.

ISBN: 978-1-897457-76-4

Section 1

Understanding
Life Systems

ISBN: 978-1-897457-76-4

1 Biomes

Every living thing needs a place to provide it with the food, water, and space that it needs to survive. We call these homes habitats, and they can be very different from one another. Habitats have different temperatures, water availability, and other things that make them suited to those who live there.

bison

After completing this unit, you will

- know that a habitat is the most comfortable home for those organisms living in it.

- know that a habitat provides organisms with food, water, air, space, and light.

- understand that there are different kinds of habitats.

I'm a plant eater. Grasslands are good places for me to live in because they provide me with a wide variety of grass.

biome: a desert
organism: cactus, camel

Vocabulary

organism: a form of life considered as a unit: an animal, a plant, a fungus, etc.

biome: a community, such as a grassland or desert, characterized by its climate and plant life

ISBN: 978-1-897457-76-4

Do you know that your backyard is a habitat for many animals and plants, such as snails and weeds? If we build a habitat for those animals or plants, they may love their new home.

Think about the questions below to see what we should consider before creating a habitat for garden snails.

- Where does a snail like to live?
- What does it eat?
- Is its habitat sunny or dark, warm or hot, wet or dry?

Read a book or surf the Internet to find out about snails and their habitat.

snail

A. Check or circle the correct answers.

Facts about
Garden Snails

Habitat

- ◯ in deserts
- ◯ in gardens
- ◯ in oceans
- ◯ in forests

- • sunny / dark
- • warm / hot
- • wet / dry

Diet

- ◯ leaves
- ◯ fruits
- ◯ insects
- ◯ cheese

B. Fill in the blanks to complete the descriptions of different kinds of biomes. Then circle the organisms that live in these habitats.

insects   life   grasses   camels   water   permafrost
coldest   elephants   treeless   plankton   precipitation
ferns   cushion plants   blue whale   hot

Different Kinds of Biomes

Grasslands

Grasslands exist throughout the Earth. These biomes are marked by sparse trees, extensive 1._____ , and a variety of small and large animals, such

Inner Mongolian grasslands in the People's Republic of China

as grasshoppers and 2._____ . There are grazing animals, burrowing animals, and their predators. Insects are abundant.

Desert

Many living things thrive in the 3._____ , dry desert. Desert plants and animals, such as cacti and 4._____ , have interesting features that help them survive in this harsh

Flora of Baja California Desert, Mexico

environment. They both have the ability to collect and store 5._____ . There is generally a smaller concentration of life forms in a desert than in other biomes.

   ISBN: 978-1-897457-76-4

Tundra

The tundra is a cold, 6._____ area; it is the 7._____ biome. The tundra has very low temperatures and very little

Tundra in Alaska

8._____ . Below a thin layer of soil is 9._____ , a layer of ground that is frozen all year long. During the short summer, the top section of the soil may thaw just long enough to allow plants to grow. Some types of plants that can take the cold and dry conditions are 10._____ and reindeer moss.

Tropical Rainforest

Tropical rainforests are found in locations that receive significant amounts of precipitation. Their locations are easily recognizable by their abundance of

The Amazon River rainforest in Peru

11._____ forms. These life forms include numerous trees, plants such as 12._____ , and an abundance of 13._____ , spiders, snakes, and other animals.

Ocean

This home covers more than half of the Earth's surface. The ocean is home to a huge variety of species, from the

The shore of the Pacific Ocean in San Francisco, California

smallest 14._____ to the largest creature on Earth, the 15._____ . It contains an incredibly diverse web of life.

ISBN: 978-1-897457-76-4

C. Read the passage. Then complete the chart.

Rainforests
in Canada!

Many think of rainforests as tropical areas close to the equator: always warm and rainy. However, there are rainforests in Canada, too, on British Columbia's Pacific coast. Called temperate rainforests, they are far from the equator and cooler than tropical rainforests; these cooler temperatures limit the types of species that can live there. Both kinds of rainforests, however, share two features: tall trees and precipitation.

In a tropical rainforest, precipitation is mostly rain. However, in Canada's temperate rainforests, precipitation is also fog, drizzle, and snow. Both types of rainforests receive a lot of precipitation. British Columbia's rainforests get 300 cm of precipitation each year, and tropical rainforests get at least 150 cm.

Tropical rainforests are home to millions of species; temperate rainforests are home to only thousands. In Canada's rainforests, giant coniferous trees dominate, and animals include the black bear, cougar, salmon, and bald eagle. Broadleaf trees dominate in tropical rainforests, and animals in Brazil's Amazon rainforest include the giant anteater, anaconda, and jaguar.

Canadian habitats are found in tundra, grasslands, forests, and deserts, but now you know there are rainforest habitats, too.

ISBN: 978-1-897457-76-4

Types of Rainforests

Tr_____ Rainforest

Location

- close to the _____

Precipitation

- at least _____ each year

Temperature

- _____

Animal

- _____

  _____

Plant

- _____

Te_____ Rainforest

Location

- far from the _____

- on the _____ side of Canada

Precipitation

- _____

Temperature

- _____

Animal

- _____

  _____

Plant

- _____

ISBN: 978-1-897457-76-4

2 Habitats and Communities

Plants and animals live together and interact in a common habitat. They depend on their environment and each other to survive. The specific needs of the living things have to be met within this habitat, or they cannot continue to exist there.

water storage ability

desert: dry environment

After completing this unit, you will

- understand that living things depend on their habitats to meet their basic needs.

- know that some environmental elements affect the ability of living things to survive in a habitat.

- know that the unique features of some living things help them survive in their habitats.

Frogs' Habitat: **Pond**

Vocabulary

habitat: the place where a plant or an animal naturally or normally lives and grows

community: interacting species sharing a common habitat

adaptation: unique features of a living thing that make it fit into a specific environment

ISBN: 978-1-897457-76-4

Have you ever visited a zoo? Zoos have different exhibits that mimic the natural habitats of animals from around the world. When you visit different exhibits at a zoo, make a record of the animals and plants that can be found there. Then describe the setting of the exhibit to show how it accommodates the needs of the animals and plants.

Tundra Exhibit
(covered with snow, very cold)

Animals: polar bears, Arctic foxes, snowy owls

Description: white hairs – blending into the snow

Plants: tiny leaves, growing close to the ground

Next time you visit a zoo, don't forget to make your own record.

A. Match each source with what it provides us. Write the letter.

A clothes/bedding

B water

C heat/light

D food

E shelter

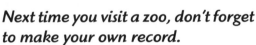

sun

vegetables

river

cotton plant

tree

B. **Choose the correct descriptions for the habitats. Write the letters. Then match each animal or plant with the habitat it is best suited to.**

(A) *areas where land and water meet; always wet; e.g. ponds and swamps*

(B) *a very dry area that is mostly hot during the day*

(C) *a place with many trees and abundant food for animals*

(D) *a place that has sparse vegetation and is cold throughout the year*

(E) *a big, open space with grass*

scorpion

Habitat

1. [ ] tundra •

2. [ ] desert •

3. [ ] wetlands •

4. [ ] forest •

5. [ ] grasslands •

• frog

• monkey

• cactus

• zebra

• mosquito

• snowy owl

• bear

• Arctic hare

• grasshopper

ISBN: 978-1-897457-76-4

C. Write the unique features of the animals and plants to show how they adapt to their habitats. Then give one more adaptive feature for each of them.

- thick, furry coat
- webbed feet to swim
- strong, fast runner
- thick stem to store water
- hard, pointed beak to crack seeds

1. wetlands _____

_____

2. forest _____

_____

3. desert _____

_____

4. tundra _____

_____

5. grasslands _____

_____

D. Read the passage. Then answer the questions.

The giant panda's only natural habitat is China's mountain forests. Pandas prefer to live alone, and the forests give them plenty of room to roam, eat, swim, climb, and sleep. Pandas are very picky eaters. While they will eat other foods, such as insects and grass, they mostly eat bamboo, which only grows at high elevations in China's mountain forests. Pandas have strong jaws and large teeth which help them crush the tough bamboo. They are also good climbers, which helps them climb up the mountains to look for food.

The Giant Panda: a Very Specific Habitat

Unfortunately, the panda's habitat is being destroyed, as people need places to live, work, log, and mine resources. Some animals such as raccoons and foxes can survive, and even thrive, in places where many people live, but pandas cannot adapt. Without a lot of bamboo in their habitat, pandas starve.

For this reason, giant pandas are considered an endangered species. Many people are helping giant pandas by working to protect and restore their natural habitat. Hopefully, the giant panda's population will increase with these efforts.

ISBN: 978-1-897457-76-4

1. What is the giant panda's natural habitat?

   (A) tropical rainforests

   (B) mountain forests

   (C) woodland forests

2. What is the giant panda's favourite food?

   (A) bamboo

   (B) foxes

   (C) insects

3. What are the unique features the giant panda has that make it suited for its habitat?

   (A) strong jaws and large teeth to crush hard bamboo

   (B) a long neck for reaching leaves high up

   (C) good at climbing

   (D) sharp claws for digging

4.
   Give a reason why we are considered an endangered species.

   _____

   _____

   _____

   _____

   _____

3 Changes to Habitats

When a habitat changes, it affects the organisms living in it. Sometimes, when there are too many changes, the living things may leave the habitat or die off. In this unit, you will learn that changes to habitats are caused by human activities or natural forces, and learn about some extinct or endangered plants and animals.

AN EXTINCT ANIMAL
"STELLER'S SEA COW"

STELLER'S SE

EXIT

After completing this unit, you will

• learn that changes to habitats can be caused by human activities or natural forces.

• know that there are extinct and endangered plants and animals around the world.

Steller's Sea Cow is a large extinct animal. Its extinction was due to overhunting.

an endangered animal – gorilla

vocabulary

deforestation: the process of removing the trees from an area of land

extinct species: a species that no longer exists

endangered species: a species that may soon become extinct

ISBN: 978-1-897457-76-4

American ginseng is a valuable plant which has been used as a traditional medicine to prevent colds and to treat diabetes and other illnesses. Due to land being cleared for farmers to plant on or builders to develop, the growth of American ginseng has been reduced significantly. Therefore, American ginseng is considered endangered. However, people have been making efforts to save this plant. Hopefully, American ginseng can be removed from the endangered species list one day.

American ginseng

A. Check the actions that could help save American ginseng.

(A) Study the needs of the American ginseng plant to see how it can be reproduced in protected environments.

(B) Dig out all the American ginseng plants and put them in a laboratory.

(C) Block off parts of a development as "Ginseng Fields" so that no houses can be built in these pockets.

(D) Make a law stating that people can only eat ginseng during New Year's celebrations.

(E)  *Educate people about American ginseng's endangered status so that they use ginseng smartly.*

B. Decide whether the habitat destruction is caused by "human" activity or "natural" forces. Then write the name of each kind of destruction.

| flooding | deforestation | farming | oil spill | wildfire |

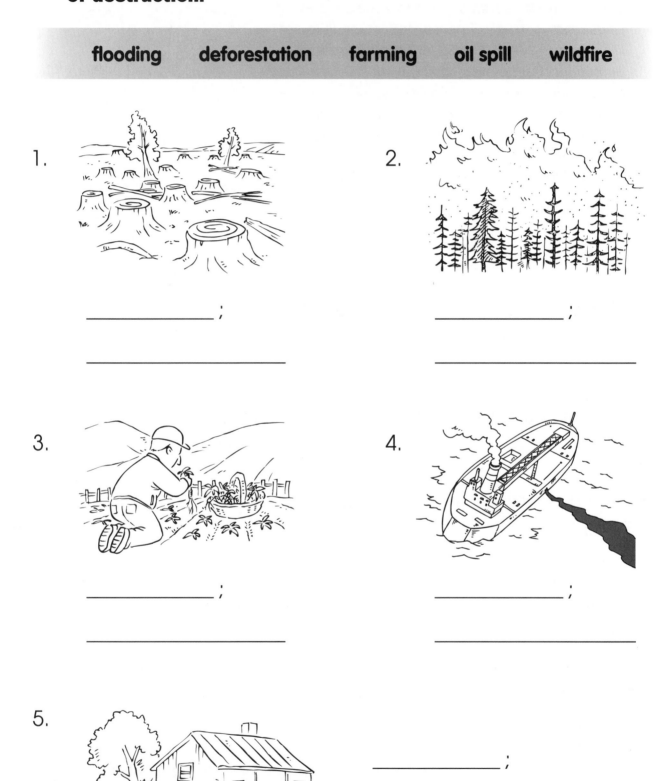

1. _____ ;

   _____

2. _____ ;

   _____

3. _____ ;

   _____

4. _____ ;

   _____

5. _____ ;

   _____

   ISBN: 978-1-897457-76-4

C. Look at the endangered animals. Match the sentences with the correct animals.

A I am gigantic. In fact, I am the largest animal in the world!

B I love the ice, but it's not always dependable!

C I like to travel in a pack and stay awake at night.

D I never need a haircut, but I do need to comb my feathers!

E I can run over 100 km per hour – as fast as a car on the highway!

F People think I am cuddly; it must be my cute, dark eyes. I live in the mountain forests of China.

Endangered Animals

1. **polar bear**

2. **blue whale**
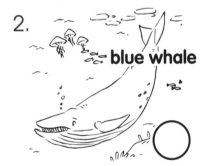

3. **panda**

4. **red wolf**

5. **bald eagle**

6. **cheetah**

D.   Read the passage. Then answer the questions.

Climate Change
and the Polar Bear

Few species can survive in the Canadian Arctic – a land of snow, ice, and frozen ground. Polar bears survive because they have adapted to this habitat: a thick layer of fat keeps them warm; and huge, rough paws give them traction on the ice. Moreover, they use sea ice as a platform from which to hunt seals, waiting at holes in the ice, which their strong sense of smell leads them to, until the seals come up for air.

However, the habitat is changing. Many people consider polar bears endangered, and this is largely a result of rising temperatures, which cause sea ice to melt earlier each spring. Early ice melts mean that polar bears have fewer days to hunt seals, forcing them to eat less while their thick layer of fat shrinks. They may die of hunger or because they cannot keep themselves warm.

Many organizations are working to protect the polar bear and its habitat. They include The World Wildlife Fund Canada and Polar Bears International. Visit their websites to see what you can do to protect the polar bear!

ISBN: 978-1-897457-76-4

1. Find pictures of the Canadian Arctic and polar bears and paste them in the boxes. Then fill in the information and answer the question.

Canadian Arctic

Habitat Description:

_____

Reasons for Habitat Change:

_____

Effects on the Environment:

_____

Polar Bear

Adaptations:

*   _____

*   _____

Threats to Survival:

*   _____

*   _____

2. Name an organization that helps protect the polar bear. Then visit its website to find an example of what it does to protect the polar bear.

_____

_____

ISBN: 978-1-897457-76-4

Experiment

Introduction

Snails can be found in our backyards. It must be that our backyards make great habitats. What will happen if the habitat of a snail changes? Will the snail respond immediately and move to a new place?

?Hypothesis

Snails respond quickly to habitat changes and move to a new place.

Steps

1. Ask an adult to help you find some snails in your backyard or in a garden. Keep the snails in a dark, cool box.

2. Place wet paper towels in the big container.

Materials

- *3 to 4 snails*
- *a big container*
- *paper towels*
- *water*
- *vinegar*
- *a dropper*

When you have finished with this experiment, take the snails back to the place where you found them.

ISBN: 978-1-897457-76-4

3. Put the snails into the container. Observe the snails for a few minutes and write down your observations.

4. Drop a few drops of vinegar on a corner of the paper towels. Observe the snails to see how they react and record your observations.

5. Repeat step 4 several times and record your observations each time.

When you drop vinegar onto the paper towels, remember to put it on the same spot each time.

Result

When the snails' habitat changes, how do the snails react?

_____

_____

_____

_____

Conclusion

The hypothesis was: _____

_____

My experiment _____ the
hypothesis.   supported / did not support

4 Our Interaction with Habitats

We depend on our habitat to provide the essentials of life. We get food, water, clothing, building materials, and medicine from our environment. In this unit, you will learn about interactions between us and our habitat and what we do to lessen the negative impacts of our activities.

After completing this unit, you will

- know that our habitat provides us with the essentials of life.
- understand that a development project has both positive and negative impacts on habitats and communities.
- understand how we try to conserve our resources.

South Town Conservation Park

a natural resource: rock

Vocabulary

resource: natural, raw material found in the environment

ecologist: a scientist who studies the relationship between organisms and their environment

ISBN: 978-1-897457-76-4

Look at the things around you. Do you know where they come from? Our habitat provides us with all the things we need to survive. Trees are a key element in our habitat and they provide us with thousands of products that we use every day. How many different tree products can you find in your house? Below is a list for your reference.

Tree Products

Food
apples
syrup

Beauty
nail polish
hair spray

Furniture
chair
table

Building Materials
lumber
plywood

Others
medicine for treating malaria
fresh air

A. Suggest something for which each natural resource below is used. Then answer the question.

1. diamond

_____

2. aluminum

_____

3. water

_____

4. gold

_____

5. wind

_____

6. oil

_____

7. Name one more natural resource and describe one of its uses.

_____ : _____

B. **Read the paragraphs and what the people say. Decide what each person is most concerned about and check that circle. Then answer the question.**

The community of St. Ferris is growing, and the community leaders propose to build more houses for the expanding population. A new housing development will be built in a woodland area.

A meeting is called in the community centre so that everyone interested in the development can present their opinions.

1. Mr. Smith, one of the community leaders, says, "We plan to build 1000 houses for families in need."

   Ⓐ positive impact on the community

   Ⓑ negative impact on the community

   Ⓒ positive impact on the habitat

2. Ms. Brant, a conservationist, says, "Ten hectares of natural habitat will be destroyed. The animals will have nowhere to go!"

   Ⓐ positive impact on the community

   Ⓑ positive impact on the habitat

   Ⓒ negative impact on the habitat

                    ISBN: 978-1-897457-76-4

3.

> The fox family will have to move out of the woodlands because they will no longer be able to find shelter or food. It will have great impact on wildlife.

an ecologist

- (A) positive impact on the community
- (B) negative impact on the habitat
- (C) negative impact on the community

4. Mr. Bell, a developer, says, "It is a good idea because it will generate more tax dollars for community improvement."

- (A) positive impact on the community
- (B) negative impact on the community
- (C) negative impact on the habitat

5. Check the ways that may help minimize any negative impacts. Then give an idea of your own.

- (A) Expand the community within the existing boundaries.
- (B) Build the new houses with high-quality materials.
- (C) Refurbish or renovate the old buildings to make good use of already developed spaces.
- (D) Abandon all housing development projects.
- (✔) _____

_____

C.   Read the passage. Then answer the questions.

Canada's Oldest National Park:

Banff National Park

Banff National Park is Canada's oldest national park. It is located in Alberta's Rocky Mountains and is made up of mountainous terrain, glaciers and ice fields, coniferous forests, and alpine meadows. Many animal and plant species call it home, including grizzly bears, cougars, moose, and pine, spruce, and fir trees.   The park protects habitats and wildlife while ensuring that people can enjoy, understand, and appreciate the natural world.

Park workers protect habitats and wildlife in many ways: they monitor species such as grizzly bears to see how human activities affect the population; they set controlled fires to encourage new plant growth; and they work to minimize and reverse the impact of human developments. For example, the Trans-Canada Highway runs through the park, and many animals have been killed crossing it. In order to minimize the highway's impact, fences have been built on both sides of the highway – along with bridges and tunnels – so that animals can cross the highway safely. However, perhaps the most important protection the park offers is this: it allows many ecosystems to function and evolve without any human interference at all.

ISBN: 978-1-897457-76-4

1. Search the Internet to find a picture of Banff National Park. Then cut and paste the picture in the box.

2. Where is Banff National Park?

_____

3. What landforms can be found in Banff National Park?

_____

_____

4. Name two animals and two plants that call Banff National Park home.

_____

_____

5. Write two things that park workers do to protect habitats and wildlife.

_____

_____

ISBN: 978-1-897457-76-4

5 Food Chains

Plants and animals depend on each other to survive in their surroundings. Each organism is part of the food chain. Energy from the sun helps plants grow, and these plants are then eaten by animals. Each part of the food chain depends on another to get energy.

After completing this unit, you will

- understand that plants use energy from the sun to grow.

- understand that animals get their energy from plants and other animals.

- understand what decomposers do.

The carrot gets energy from the sun; the bunny gets energy from the carrot; and the fox gets energy from the bunny.

Vocabulary

consumers: organisms that feed on plants or animals

producers: organisms that make their own food using energy from the sun

decomposers: organisms that break down the bodies of dead plants or animal matter into smaller pieces

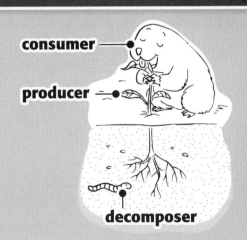

consumer

producer

decomposer

ISBN: 978-1-897457-76-4

Plants need water and nutrients from the soil as well as energy from the sun to make food in order to live and grow. These plants become food for animals which, in turn, provide food for other animals. Without plants, no animals could survive.

What would happen if there were no sun or water to feed plants?

Put some cress seeds on four paper towels and put them under different conditions to see what will happen.

Conditions

 (A) water + under the sun

 (B) water + in a dark cupboard

 (C) no water + under the sun

 (D) no water + in a dark cupboard

After a few days, take a look and see how the seeds respond to these conditions.

A. Look at the extension above. Match the results with the paper towels under different conditions. Write the letters.

1.

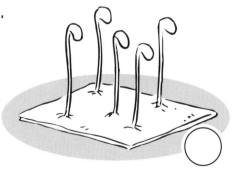

2.

3. Paper towel(s) with no change: _____

B. Fill in the blanks with the given words. Then write the role of each organism in the food chain.

decomposers   producers   consumers

Living things in a food chain can be 1._____ ,
2._____ , or 3._____ . 4._____ are plants
that make their own food using energy from the sun, water, and
air. 5._____ cannot create their own food, so they get
energy by eating animals and plants. 6._____ , such as
mushrooms and bacteria, break down dead plants and animals.
These broken down materials are then returned to the soil and
they become essential nutrients for plants.

Food Chain

An arrow in a food chain represents a transfer of energy and nutrients from one living thing to another.

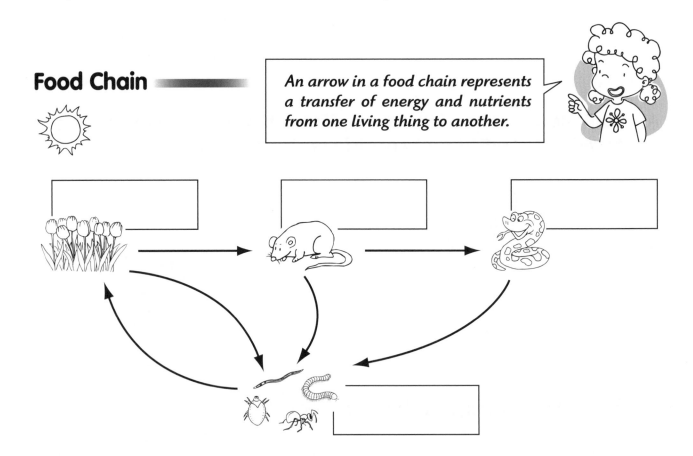

C. Decide whether each organism is a producer, consumer, or decomposer.

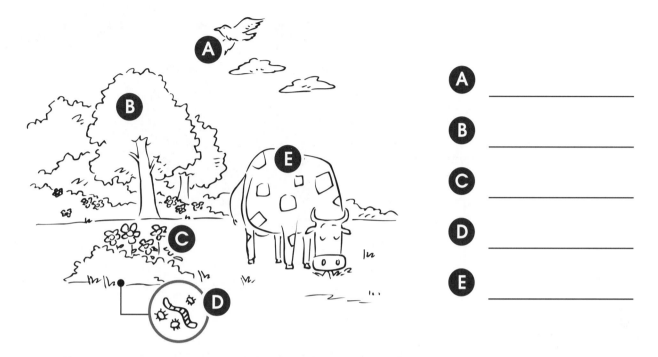

A _____

B _____

C _____

D _____

E _____

D. Fill in the missing animals or plants to complete the food chains. Then build a food chain with the given organisms.

1. grass ⟶ _____ ⟶ human

2. _____ ⟶ grasshopper ⟶ bird ⟶ _____

3. leaf ⟶ caterpillar ⟶ _____ ⟶ hawk

4.   polar bear   Arctic cod   algae   shrimp   seal

An Arctic Food Chain

ISBN: 978-1-897457-76-4

E. Read the passage. Then answer the questions.

Hi, decomposer!

Decomposers:
Nature's Recyclers

Decomposers are vital to all food chains. They are nature's recyclers, breaking down dead plant and animal matter into essential nutrients and returning those nutrients to the soil so that producers can use them to make food. Decomposers do their work by producing chemicals, called enzymes, to digest the dead material.

Many decomposers are microorganisms, which can only be seen under a microscope. These decomposers include bacteria, some of which can be found inside our bodies, helping us digest our food, and fungi, which you can see in the form of mushrooms growing on dead trees or as mould growing on old bread. Most worms are also considered decomposers and are a great addition to your backyard compost heap.

Next time you see a piece of forgotten, mouldy bread in a dark corner of a cupboard or an earthworm squirming across your front lawn, think about this: without decomposers, dead plant and animal matter would cover the Earth, from forests to sidewalks to your own backyard!

   ISBN: 978-1-897457-76-4

1. Circle the correct words.

   a. Decomposers are **important / not important** to all food chains.

   b. Decomposers produce **waste / enzymes** to digest dead material.

   c. Bacteria are **decomposers / fungi** that are able to break down dead material.

   d. Without decomposers, the Earth would be covered in **nutrients / waste** .

2. Give three examples of decomposers.

   _____

3. Why do decomposers play an important role in all food chains?

   _____

   _____

4. Which of the following are evidence of decomposers at work? Check the correct answers.

   (A) rotten lettuce

   (B) mushrooms growing on dead trees

   (C) broken glass

   (D) growing sunflowers

   (E) decaying leaves

   (F) mouldy bread

mould

6 What Animals Eat

Have you seen a cow eat meat or a lion eat grass? Probably not! Different animals have different diets. In this unit, you will learn about how animals can be classified by what they eat – as herbivores, carnivores, or omnivores.

After completing this unit, you will

- know that animals have different diets and that they are classified into three groups accordingly.

- understand that organisms get energy from other organisms through the food chain.

> *Since you are an omnivore, you should eat some vegetables with your meal to keep yourself healthy.*

herbivores

We love grass.

herbivore: an animal that eats plants only

carnivore: an animal that eats animals only

omnivore: an animal that eats both plants and animals

ISBN: 978-1-897457-76-4

Animals have specialized teeth to help them eat. Take a closer look at the teeth of a lion and a giraffe. You can see that lions have sharp and long teeth, called fangs, for tearing meat. These sharp teeth are like knives, which are perfect for lions because they are meat eaters. How about the teeth of a giraffe? Giraffes have big, flat teeth which are perfect for grinding their favourite food – leaves. Giraffes are plant eaters.

Look in a mirror and check your teeth to see what kind you have. Are you a meat eater or plant eater?

A. Check the animals that are meat eaters. Then answer the questions.

1.

2. Name one feature the meat eaters have in common.

_____

3. Look at the animals that you did not check. What do they eat?

_____

B. Fill in the blanks to complete the paragraph. Then classify the animals.

| herbivores | omnivores | consumers | carnivores | producers |

1._____ , mostly plants, are always at the beginning of a food chain. Next are the 2._____ , which are animals. Based on their eating habits, animals are classified as one of three types of consumers: animals that eat plants are 3._____ ; animals that eat other animals are 4._____ ; and animals that eat both plants and animals are 5._____ . 6._____ are always directly linked to the producer in a food chain.

7. **Types of Animals**

A _____

B _____

C _____

D _____

E. _____

ISBN: 978-1-897457-76-4

C. Read what Jenny says. Complete the food chain with the given animals and label each of them as an omnivore, a herbivore, or a carnivore. Then answer the questions.

Every level of a food chain gets energy from the level below it and gives energy to the level above it, so every level is dependent on the level below for survival.

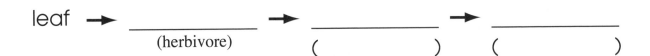

1. 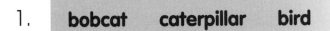 **bobcat   caterpillar   bird**

   leaf ➡ _____ ➡ _____ ➡ _____

           (herbivore)   (   )   (   )

2. **lizard   grasshopper   snake**

   grass ➡ _____ ➡ _____ ➡ _____

         (   )   (   )   (   )

3. What would happen to a food chain if the producers disappeared?

   _____

4. Look at the food chain in question 2. What would happen if the lizard was not there? Explain.

   _____

   _____

D.   Read the passage. Then answer the questions.

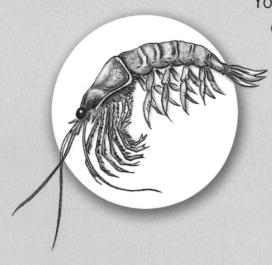

What Makes a Blue Whale Big?

The blue whale is the largest animal on Earth. It can weigh 172 tonnes, about the weight of 25 male African elephants! A newborn weighs only about 2.7 tonnes, but can gain up to 90 kilograms each day. That is like gaining the weight of a professional basketball player each day!

Can you guess what a blue whale eats to get this big? You might think they eat other whales, dolphins, giant fish, squid, or octopi, but a blue whale's favourite food is a tiny creature called krill. Krill look like shrimp, but most grow to be only the size of a safety pin. An adult blue whale can eat up to 40 million of them a day, bringing huge amounts of krill-filled water into its mouth and filtering it until only krill, and the occasional fish or squid, are left to swallow.

ISBN: 978-1-897457-76-4

1. Write **T** for true and **F** for false.

   a. An African elephant weighs as much
      as 25 blue whales.   _____

   b. A newborn blue whale weighs about
      2.7 tonnes.   _____

   c. A blue whale's favourite foods are
      dolphins, giant fish, squid, and octopi.   _____

   d. Blue whales are carnivores.   _____

2. What is the blue whale's favourite food? How much can a
   blue whale eat in a day?

   _____

   _____

3. Complete the Antarctic food chain.

krill	plankton (tiny plants)	blue whale

   _____ ➔ _____ ➔ _____

4. What would happen if plankton were missing in the food
   chain?

   _____

   _____

ISBN: 978-1-897457-76-4

Experiment

Introduction

Have you ever wondered if birds like foods other than bird seed? Do birds like lettuce or crackers as well?

My dog, Teddy, likes chicken and I like cheese and cookies. All of us have our favourite foods.

Hypothesis

Birds prefer seeds to other kinds of food.

Materials

- *an egg carton*
- *a cup of bird seed*
- *a cup of crumbled crackers*
- *a cup of chopped lettuce*
- *a pair of scissors*
- *three pieces of string*

Steps

1. Cut the top off the egg carton with a pair of scissors.

2. Tie two pieces of string tightly around the egg carton.

 ISBN: 978-1-897457-76-4

3. Tie each end of the third piece of string to one of the loops made by the first two strings.

hanger

bird feeder

4. Fill four egg cups with seeds, four with crackers, and four with lettuce, and hang the bird feeder on a tree.

5. Check the feeder every day for a week and make a table to record the amount of each kind of food eaten. Refill the cups after checking.

Result

Do birds eat different kinds of food or do they only like seeds?

_____

_____

Conclusion

The hypothesis was: _____

_____

My experiment _____ the
hypothesis.   supported / did not support

Try to complete this review in **30 minutes**.

30 minutes

This review consists of six sections, from A to F. The marks for each question are shown in parentheses. The circle at the bottom right corner is for the marks you get in each section. An overall record is on the last page of the review.

A. Write T for true and F for false.

1. A forest is a place with many trees and abundant food for animals. (**2**)   _____

2. Producers cannot create their own food, so they get energy by eating other animals and plants. (**2**)   _____

3. Sheep are omnivores. (**2**)

    _____

4. Grasslands, deserts, tundra, tropical rainforests, and oceans are some of Earth's major biomes. (**2**)

    _____

forest

8

ISBN: 978-1-897457-76-4

B. Do the matching.

1.
(2)

2.
(2)

3.
(2)

4.
(2)

5.
(2)

6.
(2)

- destruction of habitat caused by natural forces

- one of the major biomes

- an endangered animal

- producers; make their own food

- herbivore; eats plants only

- destruction of habitat caused by human activities

C. Circle the habitat that the animal is adapted to. Describe a unique feature of the animal to show how it adapts to that habitat.

1.

   Habitat: **grasslands / forest**

   Feature: _____

   _____

2.   Habitat: **tundra / wetlands**

   Feature: _____

   _____

D. Answer the questions.

1. Name two human activities that cause habitat destruction. **(4)**

   _____

2. Name two natural forces that cause habitat destruction. **(4)**

   _____

3. If a development project is planned where a forest is, what might be the impacts on the habitat and the community? **(6)**

   _____

   _____

   _____

   _____

24

ISBN: 978-1-897457-76-4

E. **Describe the role of each type of organism in the food chain and give an example of an organism that has that role. Then label the food chain with each organism's role.**

1. **producer** (6)

   _____

   example: _____

2. **consumer** (6)

   _____

   example: _____

3. **decomposer** (6)

   _____

   example: _____

4.
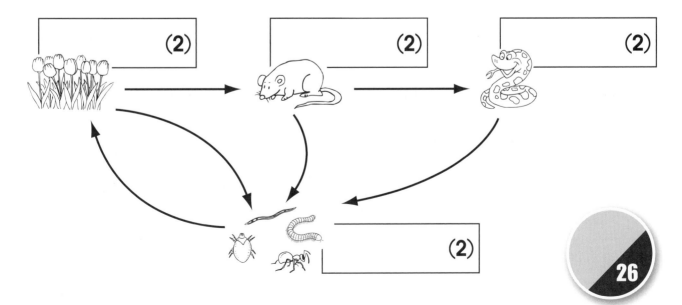

Food Chain

(2)   (2)   (2)

(2)

26

ISBN: 978-1-897457-76-4

F. **Build a food chain with the organisms in each group and identify the biome where the food chain would be found. Then answer the questions.**

Group 1	Group 2	Group 3
lemming	deer	seal
lichen	fern	fish
Arctic fox	cougar	plankton
snowy owl		white shark

1. **Group 1** a food chain in the _____ biome **(6)**

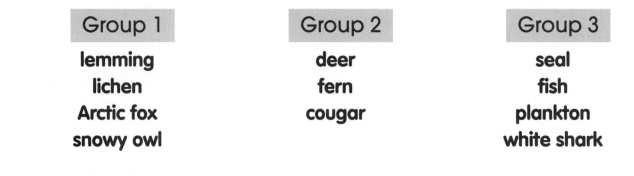

2. **Group 2** a food chain in the _____ biome **(6)**

3. **Group 3** a food chain in the _____ biome **(6)**

4. What would happen if ferns in Group 2 were missing? **(6)**

_____

5. What does an arrow in a food chain represent? **(6)**

_____

_____

30

ISBN: 978-1-897457-76-4

My Record

Section **A**	8
Section **B**	12
Sections **C, D**	24
Section **E**	26
Section **F**	30

Total

100

80-100

Great work! You really understand your science stuff! Research your favourite science topics at the library or on the Internet to find out more about the topics related to this section. Keep challenging yourself to learn more!

60-79

Good work! You understand some basic concepts, but try reading through the units again to see whether you can master the material! Go over the questions that you had trouble with to make sure you know the correct answers.

below 60

You can do much better! Try reading over the units again. Ask your parents or teachers any questions you might have. Once you feel confident that you know the material, try the review again. Science is exciting, so don't give up!

The Explorer

The ocean has been called the final frontier because so much of it has yet to be explored and may never be explored. There are countless unnamed and undiscovered species, relationships between species that are not understood, and entire ecosystems that have never been studied by scientists. In short, the ocean is a mystery, but many have tried to explore its depths, including the famous ocean explorer, Jacques-Yves Cousteau.

Jacques-Yves Cousteau was born in France on June 11, 1910. He studied the ocean and its organisms extensively and is credited by many as a pioneer of marine conservation. Cousteau helped make ocean exploration possible by co-inventing what is now called the Self Contained Underwater Breathing Apparatus, SCUBA, in 1943. He also made underwater movies, wrote many books, and hosted television shows that featured his explorations and discoveries in order to teach people about the wonders of the oceans and why they need to be protected.

ISBN: 978-1-897457-76-4

Cool Science Facts

1 Which is older – a cockroach or a dinosaur?

2 Do all animals drink water?

3 How does a snake eat things that are so much bigger than itself?

4 Why do some animals have whiskers?

5 Do Arctic polar bears feel cold?

Find the answers on the next page.

ISBN: 978-1-897457-76-4

Cool Science Facts

1 Scientists found cockroach fossils that are about 300 million years old. That is 70 million years older than the oldest dinosaur! Maybe cockroaches outlived dinosaurs because they can eat almost anything and can survive for a long time without food and water.

> My ancestors lived many years before yours!

2 All animals need water to survive but they get it in different ways. Frogs and freshwater fish absorb water into their bodies through their skin.

3

ISBN: 978-1-897457-76-4

A snake does not chew but swallows its prey whole. It has flexible, stretchy jaws that allow it to open its mouth wider than its own head. Snakes also have flexible ribs so their bodies can expand to accommodate large prey.

4 Animals use whiskers to sense and make judgments about their surroundings. Whiskers are particularly useful for cats to judge spaces in the dark. A cat can tell if an opening is large enough for it to get through before it ventures out.

5 Polar bears have blubber underneath their thick fur coats, keeping them insulated. They also have black skin to absorb as much heat as possible from the sun. Polar bears are so well adapted to cold weather that they sometimes get too hot and need to go for a swim to cool down.

ISBN: 978-1-897457-76-4

ISBN: 978-1-897457-76-4

Section **2**

Understanding
Structures and
Mechanisms

ISBN: 978-1-897457-76-4

1 Machines in the Past

People have used simple machines for a long time. During the Middle Ages, simple machines were used to build, protect, and attack medieval castles. In this unit, you will see how machines have made work easier for people in different societies throughout time.

After completing this unit, you will

- understand how simple machines were used in the past.
- understand how simple machines were used to defend castles.

> It is difficult for me to move in this heavy suit of armour, so my page heaves me onto my horse using a pulley system.

Vocabulary

inclined plane: a slanting surface connecting a lower level to a higher level

lever: a stiff bar that moves around a fixed point

fulcrum: a point on which a lever pivots

wheel: a circular machine that turns around an axle

inclined plane

inclined plane

ISBN: 978-1-897457-76-4

An inclined plane is an interesting simple machine because it is simply a flat surface raised at an angle, but it is used in different forms and for various purposes. A ramp is an example of an inclined plane that helps in lifting and moving heavy objects with less effort. Some scientists also believe that an internal ramp system was used to build the Great Pyramids in Egypt.

Nowadays, people have different machines such as slides, roller coasters, stairs, and windmills that use inclined planes. Can you find more examples of inclined planes around you?

inclined plane

A. Unscramble the letters to name the early simple machines. Then fill in the blanks.

1.

   path

   Simple machine: _____ plane
   _{dnincile}

   Moving a heavy load up an inclined plane

   is _____ than lifting it up.
   easier / harder

2.

   siege tower

   Simple machine: _____ and _____
   ehwel   lxae

   It is much _____ to move a heavy load
   easier / harder

   on wheels than it is to drag it over the ground.

B. Complete the passage and label the diagram with the given words. Then put the pictures in order.

sling	rope	fulcrum	lever	weight	rock

How a Catapult* Works

The 1._____ of a catapult was a long beam fixed at a

point called the 2._____ .   A weight was hung on one

end of the beam. A very strong piece of material made into a

3._____ was attached on the other end.

Soldiers put a large 4._____ inside the sling and used

5._____ to pull down this side of the long beam. When it

was let go, the heavy 6._____ crashed down. This made

the other end of the lever fly up,

throwing the rock towards

the castle.

> *A catapult was a simple machine that used a lever to shoot a rock into the air to break a castle wall during an attack.

7.

Medieval Catapult

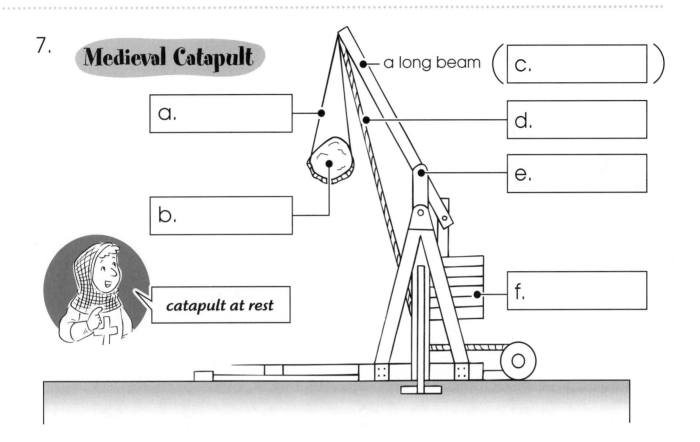

a long beam

a.

b.

c.

d.

e.

f.

catapult at rest

8. Put the pictures in order from 1 to 4 to show how a catapult works.

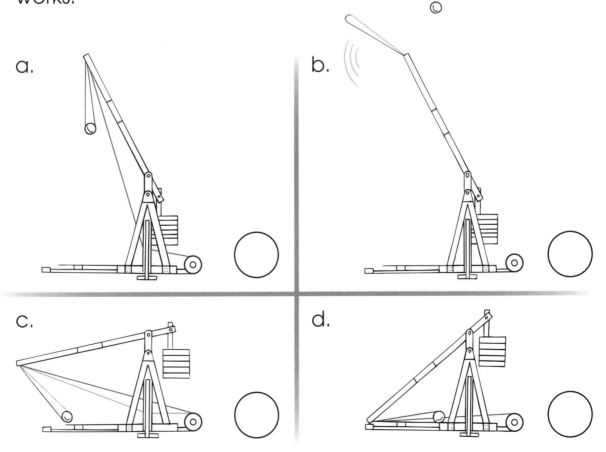

a.

b.

c.

d.

ISBN: 978-1-897457-76-4

C. Read the passage. Then answer the questions.

Castle Drawbridge - a Simple Machine

The castle drawbridge was lowered to allow people into the castle through its single entrance and raised to keep attackers out during a siege.

Most worked by using two long pieces of wood, which were levers. They hung above the drawbridge, attached to it by ropes (or by much stronger and longer-lasting chains). Each one was fixed at the castle wall, which was the fulcrum. Behind the castle wall, ropes (or chains) were attached to these pieces of wood. When guards pulled on the ropes, the bridge was lifted.

Weights were also attached to the lever, which made lifting the heavy bridge easier.

ISBN: 978-1-897457-76-4

1. Label the drawbridge diagram with the given words.

fulcrum
rope
lever
weight

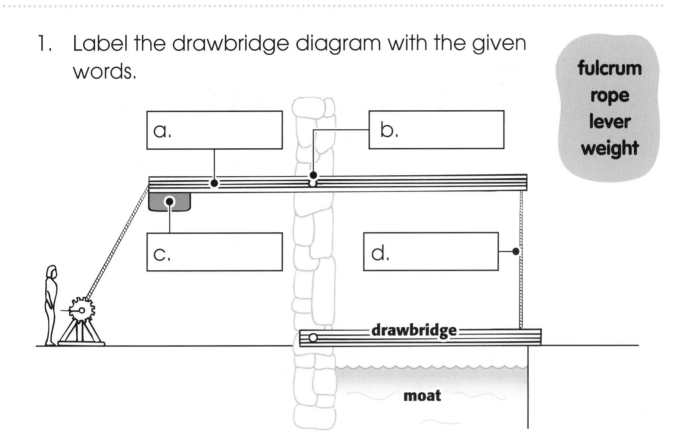

a.

b.

c.

d.

drawbridge

moat

2. Draw the weight, lever, ropes, and drawbridge to show a drawbridge being raised. Then draw arrows to show the direction of the lever's movement.

How a Drawbridge Works

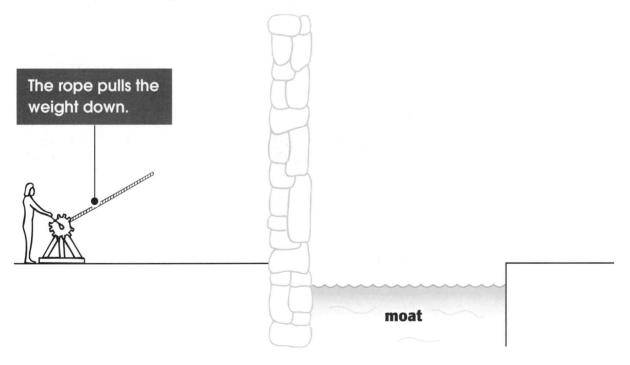

The rope pulls the weight down.

moat

ISBN: 978-1-897457-76-4

2 Simple Machines

Machines can be very complex, with many moving parts. They can also be simple, with few or no moving parts. These are known as simple machines. In this unit, you will see how simple machines multiply our force and how they help make our work easier.

After completing this unit, you will

- know some rules to follow when working with simple machines.

- understand the ways in which some simple machines work.

lever

Katie, I can lift you up easily with the help of this simple machine.

Six Classical Simple Machines

 lever

 wheel and axle

 pulley

 inclined plane

 wedge

 screw

Vocabulary

simple machine: a device that changes the direction or magnitude of a force

wedge: a simple machine with at least one slanting side and a sharp edge

ISBN: 978-1-897457-76-4

Have you ever wondered why it is easy to cut things with knives and saws? When you take a closer look at knives and saws, you may find that they are simple machines – wedges. A wedge has a wide end and a sharp end which work together to split things.

Mom, I know that a sharp knife is safer than a dull one. A dull knife can be much harder to control than a sharp one because we must use more force with a dull knife to make it cut.

A. Check the rules that we should follow when we work with machines.

Rules to Follow When We Work with Machines:

(A) Wear safety goggles and protective clothing if needed.

(B) Keep yourself busy at all times.

(C) Tie long hair back.

(D) Remove loose jewellery when working with gears or pulleys.

(E) Wear bright-coloured shoes.

(F) Make sure pulleys and gears are fastened securely before testing them with a load.

B. Read the experiments and guess what will happen. Circle the correct answers.

1.

Pulling Power

A Get two friends to pull two brooms apart while you try to keep the brooms together.

B Thread a rope around the two brooms. Get two friends to try to pull the brooms apart while you pull the free end of the rope to push the brooms together.

Result

A You were **able / unable** to keep the brooms together.

B You were **able / unable** to keep the brooms together.

Conclusion

When the rope is threaded between the brooms, it acts as a group of **pulleys / screws**. The more times the rope loops back and forth, the **greater / smaller** the force is magnified. Therefore, your force in **B** was **increased / decreased** by the "pulleys".

ISBN: 978-1-897457-76-4

2.

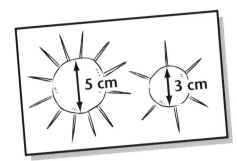

- Flatten two pieces of modelling clay to make two wheels – one 5 cm across and the other 3 cm across.

- Stick 12 toothpicks around the edge of the big wheel and 6 toothpicks around the small one.

- Push a pencil through the centre of each wheel.

- Squeeze the clay tightly around the pencil so that both the wheel and the axle turn together.

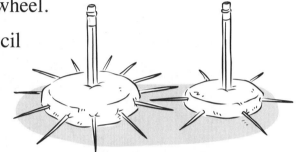

- Place both wheels flat on a table so that their toothpicks interlock.

- Use the pencil to spin the large wheel in a clockwise direction once.

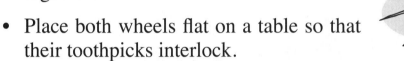

Result

The small wheel spins in a **clockwise / counter-clockwise** direction when the big wheel spins in a clockwise direction. The small wheel spins **faster / slower** than the big one.

Conclusion

The toothpicks are like teeth on a wheel. Interlocking toothed wheels of different sizes causes the wheels to move at different **speeds / angles** .

The **small / large** wheel makes more turns each time the large wheel turns. Therefore, when we spin the large wheel, the small wheel will move at a **faster / slower** speed.

C. Read the passage. Then answer the questions.

Eloise
and the Scarf

Eloise is strolling through the park when she notices a girl crying. "What's wrong?" she asks. The girl cries, "I lost my scarf, and when I found it, it's stuck under this rock!" Eloise knows she can help. She finds a small rock and sets it close to the big rock. Next, she finds a long stick. She puts the stick between the ground and the big rock and rests it on the small rock so that the stick slants upwards. She pushes down on the end of the stick, but nothing happens. Then she finds a longer stick, and tries again. This time, she lifts the big rock and it rolls away. The girl picks up her scarf. "Thank you," she says. "You're welcome, but you should thank levers*," Eloise laughs.

Lever

load   effort

fulcrum

*lever: a rigid bar that turns on a fulcrum to transfer a force from one place to another

ISBN: 978-1-897457-76-4

1. Check the picture that shows how Eloise rescued the scarf from the rock. Then describe each element in the picture with the terms that we use for levers.

(A)

(B)

Description: _____

_____

_____

2. Check the correct sentences.

(A) You can move a heavy weight with little effort when you use a lever.

(B) You need to apply more effort over a longer distance to move a load with a lever.

(C) The longer a lever is, the greater the force it can transfer from the effort to the load.

3. Give an example of a machine that contains the two simple machines mentioned to make our work easier.

a. lever and wedge   _____

b. lever and gears   _____

3 Gears

Do you ride a bicycle? Bike handlebars, pedals, and the wheels and axles are parts you should be familiar with. A bike also has special, toothed wheels called gears that transfer your effort to the bicycle's movement. In this unit, you will learn about how gears work and see how a gear system on a bicycle works.

> *I can go fast on a flat surface by using the largest gear on the front chain ring and the smallest gear on the rear wheel.*

largest gear

smallest gear

After completing this unit, you will

- understand how a simple gear train works.
- understand how gears help power bicycles.

Vocabulary

speed: a measure of the rate of motion

force: the capacity to do work or cause physical change

gear: a toothed machine part that interlocks with another toothed part to transmit motion, or to change speed or direction

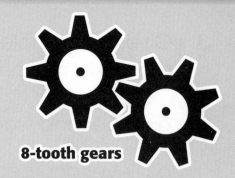

8-tooth gears

ISBN: 978-1-897457-76-4

Do you know that there are many things around us that use gears? Gears can be found in everything from cars to clocks. Get your parents' approval before checking the listed items in your house to see whether or not they use gears.

gears

Items with Gears...

◯ clock   ◯ can opener

◯ DVD player   ◯ hand egg beater

A. Follow the directions to make cardboard gears. Use them to try out the activities in this unit.

1. Trace the gears onto a white sheet of paper.

2. Use this as a stencil to make gears out of heavy, thick cardboard.

3. Cut out the cardboard gears. Ask your parents for help if needed.

After doing the activities on the following pages, save your gears for the experiment on pages 78 and 79.

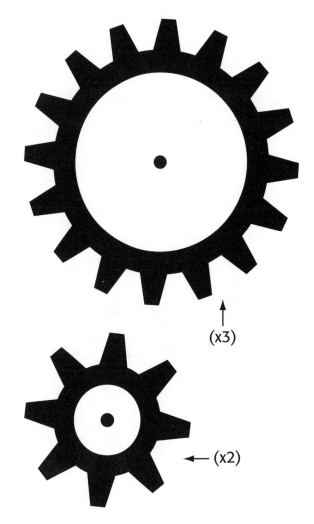

(x3)

(x2)

B. Set up and label the 16-tooth gears as below. Then draw arrows to show the directions and answer the questions.

Activity 1

Use brass fasteners to fasten the gears onto a piece of cardboard; make sure the gears interlock.

1.

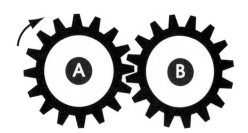   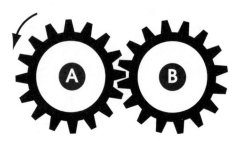

Ⓐ turns clockwise

Ⓑ turns a._____

Ⓐ turns counter-clockwise

Ⓑ turns b._____

2. Does a gear change the direction of motion? _____

Activity 2

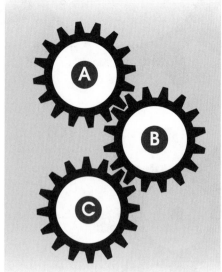

3.

Gears	A	B	C
Direction			

4. If another gear is attached to C, in what direction will it turn when A turns clockwise?

_____

ISBN: 978-1-897457-76-4

C. Set up the gears as below. Explore what happens when gears of different sizes are used together. Then answer the questions.

Activity 1

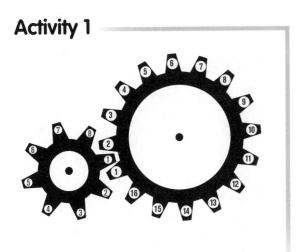

Activity 2

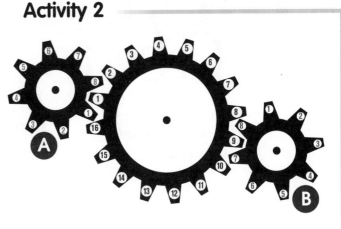

Activity 1   *The big gear turns once in a clockwise direction.*

1. How many times does the small gear turn?   _____

2. Is the speed of the small gear faster or slower than the big gear?   _____

3. In what direction does the small gear turn?   _____

Activity 2   *The big gear turns once in a counter-clockwise direction.*

4. How many times does gear B turn and in what direction?

_____

5. Are the speeds of gears A and B the same? Do they move in the same direction?

_____

_____

D. Read the passage. Then answer the questions.

A **Bicycle's** Gears

> *Today, biking uphill is much easier.*

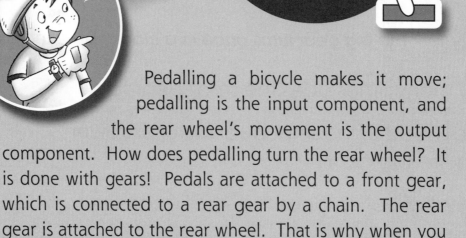

40 teeth

20 teeth

Pedalling a bicycle makes it move; pedalling is the input component, and the rear wheel's movement is the output component. How does pedalling turn the rear wheel? It is done with gears! Pedals are attached to a front gear, which is connected to a rear gear by a chain. The rear gear is attached to the rear wheel. That is why when you pedal, the rear wheel turns.

Most bicycles have front and rear gears of different sizes that are changed for different situations. For **biking on level ground**, a large front gear (e.g. 50 teeth) and a small rear gear (e.g. 15 teeth) are best. This way, each turn of your pedals rotates the rear wheel more than once, making you move quickly, though you need lots of leg strength. For **biking uphill**, a smaller front gear (e.g. 20 teeth) and a larger rear gear (e.g. 40 teeth) are best. This way, the rider turns the pedals more often for each full rotation of the rear wheel, making it easy to pedal, though difficult to move quickly.

ISBN: 978-1-897457-76-4

1. Write **T** for true and **F** for false.

    a. Gears make a bicycle move. _____

    b. The input component of a bicycle is pedalling. _____

    c. A chain is used to connect the front gear and the rear gear of a bicycle. _____

    d. A small front gear and a large rear gear are best for biking uphill. _____

2. Match the correct descriptions with each diagram.

front (50 teeth) **and rear** (15 teeth) **front** (20 teeth) **and rear** (40 teeth)	**move slowly** **move fast**	**easy to pedal** **hard to pedal**

<table>
<tr><td>Biking on Level Ground</td><td>Biking Uphill</td></tr>
<tr><td>• _____</td><td>• _____</td></tr>
<tr><td>• _____</td><td>• _____</td></tr>
<tr><td>• _____</td><td>• _____</td></tr>
</table>

ISBN: 978-1-897457-76-4

Introduction

Gears are versatile and can help produce a range of movement that can be used to control the speed of action. When several gears are connected to make a gear train, do the gears of the same size move at the same speed even if there are gears between them?

Hypothesis

The speeds of rotation of gears of the same size are the same, even if there is another gear between them.

Materials

- *cardboard gears*
- *pins*
- *markers*
- *cardboard*

Steps

1. Have the cardboard gears (two 16-tooth and one 8-tooth) from unit 3 ready.

2. On each gear, mark one of the teeth with a marker.

3. Pin the centre of each gear on a sheet of cardboard as shown on the next page.

ISBN: 978-1-897457-76-4

a mark

Make sure the 16-tooth gears are pinned with the marks pointing at the same direction.

4. Turn gear A and observe the speeds of rotation of gears B and C.

5. Compare the speeds of gears B and C with A.

Speeds of the Gears   *(faster than/slower than/the same as)*

B is _____ A.

C is _____ A.

Result

Did gear A and gear C rotate at the same speed?

_____

Conclusion

The hypothesis was: _____

_____

My experiment _____ the
hypothesis.   supported / did not support

4 Gears around Us

There are many machines that use gears all around us. We use different types of gears to make our jobs easier. In this unit, you will learn how different types of gears work and how they change the speed, direction, and motion of moving objects.

Gears make my work much easier.

After completing this unit, you will
- be able to identify some everyday machines that use gears.
- understand that there are different kinds of gear systems, including rack and pinion systems.

gears

drill: a compound machine

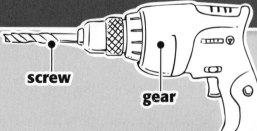

screw

gear

Vocabulary

simple machine: a device that changes the direction or magnitude of a force

compound machine: a machine made up of two or more simple machines

ISBN: 978-1-897457-76-4

Take a closer look at a can opener, and you will see that it is made up of several simple machines. To use a can opener, you squeeze two levers together. This action pushes the wedge into the can. When you turn the handle, the wheel and axle turn the wedge to cut the lid away from the can with the help of a pair of gears.

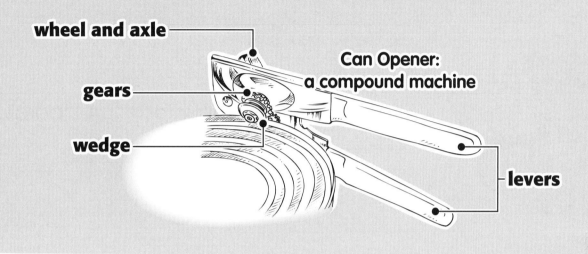

wheel and axle

gears

wedge

Can Opener: a compound machine

levers

A. Name the simple machines that are used with gears to make each compound machine.

1.

egg beater

simple machines used:

_____

_____

2.

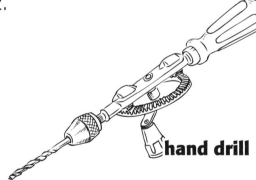

hand drill

simple machines used:

_____

_____

B.   Name the gears. Then fill in the blanks.

| bevel gears   worm gear | one   two   shafts   direction |
| idler gear   spur gears | same   worm   one   two |

1.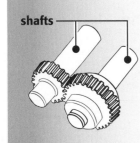

   shafts

   - s_____ g_____
   - straight   teeth,   mounted   on   parallel
     _____
   - operate in _____ plane

2.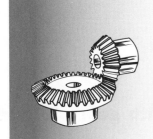

   - b_____ g_____
   - change the _____ of movement
   - operate in _____ planes

3.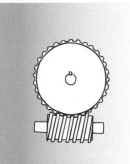

   - a w_____ g_____ system
   - a combination of a circular gear and a
     _____ gear
   - operates in _____ planes

4.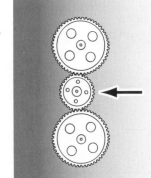

   - an i_____ g_____
   - used to keep two connected gears rotating
     in the _____ direction
   - operates in _____ plane

ISBN: 978-1-897457-76-4

C. Draw arrows to show how the gear turns. Then write and check the correct answers.

A Rack and Pinion System

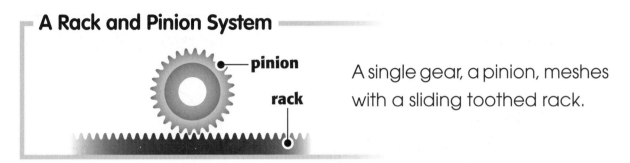

pinion

rack

A single gear, a pinion, meshes with a sliding toothed rack.

1.

The rack moves to the left.

The rack moves to the right.

2.

A rack and pinion system converts rotary motion to _____ motion.

linear / dynamic

3. Check the examples of machines that use a rack and pinion system.

- (A) the rear wheel of a bicycle
- (B) windshield wipers in cars
- (C) a clock pendulum
- (D) the pointer in a bathroom scale
- (E) the wheel of a wheelbarrow

D.   Read Celine's activity sheet. Then answer the questions.

Science and Technology   Name: *Celine Winter*

Build a Gear System

You will need 2 or more gears.

Objective: to build a gear system
of two or more gears
to achieve a goal

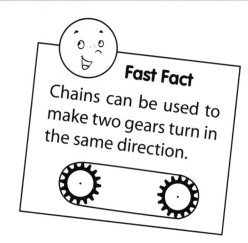

Fast Fact
Chains can be used to make two gears turn in the same direction.

Plan   *My plan is to make a ballet show with two
ballerina dolls; each doll will stand on a gear.
Turning one of the dolls will make the other doll
turn and they will perform a show.*

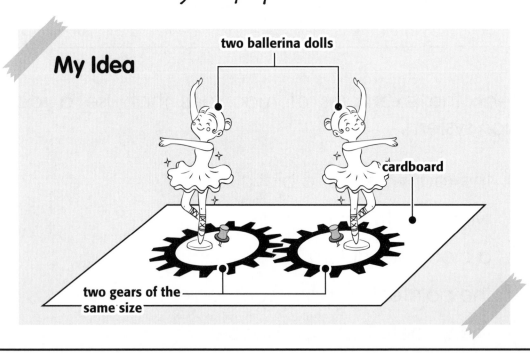

two ballerina dolls

My Idea

cardboard

two gears of the
same size

ISBN: 978-1-897457-76-4

1. In Celine's design, do the ballerina dolls spin

    a. in the same direction? _____

    b. at the same speed? _____

2. If Celine wants to have the ballerina dolls turn in the same direction, in which two ways can she do it? Write about each way and draw a diagram with gears to support your ideas.

Way 1

_____

_____

_____

Way 2

_____

_____

_____

3. If Celine wants to have the ballerina dolls turn at different speeds, what can she do? Write about it and draw a diagram.

_____

_____

_____

5 Pulleys Everywhere

We use pulleys every day and pulleys can be found everywhere. In this unit, you will identify pulleys that are used in our daily lives and understand how a pulley works and how to use one.

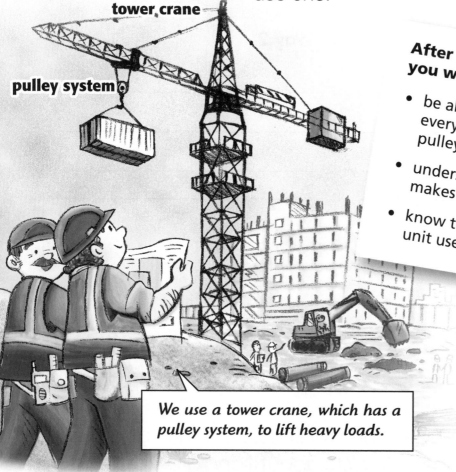

tower crane

pulley system

We use a tower crane, which has a pulley system, to lift heavy loads.

After completing this unit, you will

- be able to identify many everyday machines that use pulleys.
- understand why a pulley makes lifting a load easier.
- know that a newton (N) is a unit used to measure force.

pulley

load

Vocabulary

pulley: a simple machine consisting of a grooved wheel and a rope that runs over the wheel

load: a weight that is supported or lifted

ISBN: 978-1-897457-76-4

Pulleys are important simple machines that are widely used in our daily lives. In the Middle Ages, people used pulleys to lift heavy stone blocks to build the walls of castles.

Cranes, like the one shown in the picture, were used to build large, stone buildings in the Middle Ages. The crane was powered by men running inside the two huge wheels.

pulley

A. Check the examples of pulleys found at home.

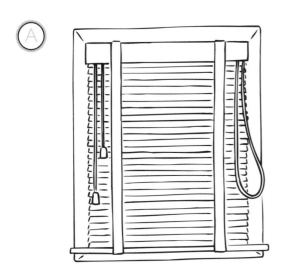

(A)

(B)

(C) garage door

(D) egg beater

(E) portable vacuum cleaner

(F) retractable clothesline

B. Trace the arrows to show the movement. Then label the diagram.

A Pulley

1.

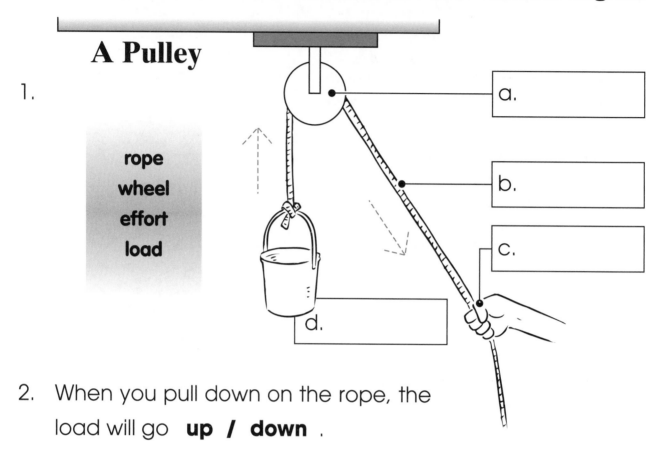

rope
wheel
effort
load

| a. |
| b. |
| c. |
| d. |

2. When you pull down on the rope, the
    load will go **up / down** .

**C. Ted did experiments on lifting weights with
and without the help of a pulley. Look at
his record. Then answer the questions.**

Force Needed to Lift a Weight		
Weight	Without a Pulley	With a Pulley
10 N*	10 N	10 N
30 N	30 N	30 N
50 N	50 N	50 N

Without a pulley

With a pulley

The unit for measuring force is newton (N).

 This little device is used to measure force.

ISBN: 978-1-897457-76-4

1. How much force is needed to lift a weight of 50 N

   a. without using a pulley? _____

   b. with a pulley? _____

2. Predict how much force is needed to lift a weight of 80 N

   a. without using a pulley. _____

   b. with a pulley. _____

3. The amount of force needed to lift a load in both cases is

   _____ , but you may find that it is _____ to
   the same / different   easier / harder

   pull down than it is to pull up.

4. A pulley lets you use your _____ to lift a load.
   weight / height

5.
   > If we need to get a bucket of water from a well, how can we use
   > a pulley to make it easier to lift the bucket? Show your idea by
   > drawing it.

D. Read the passage. Then answer the questions.

Everyday Pulleys

The uses of pulleys are endless. In **recreation**, pulleys are used to keep rock climbers safe in indoor gyms. They are essential parts in many weight-lifting exercise machines. Sailboats use many fixed and movable pulleys to raise, lower, and change the position of sails. In **construction**, pulleys are used in cranes, which move construction materials vertically and horizontally. Pulleys are important in **shipping** as well. Heavy loads are lifted and lowered using cranes and forklifts, both of which use pulleys. Pulleys are also used in **building maintenance** to lift and lower hanging scaffolding, which provides a moving platform for workers who paint or repair the exteriors of tall buildings or wash windows. At **home**, pulleys are used in garage doors, window blinds, and clotheslines. Some **restaurants** have mini-elevators called dumbwaiters that use a pulley system to move food from the kitchen to the dining floors.

No, Boots! That pulley system is for opening and closing the blinds, not for playing!

ISBN: 978-1-897457-76-4

1. Give an example of how pulleys are used in each area mentioned in the passage.

Area	**Tools with Pulleys** (function)
• in buildings	elevators – allow easy access to all floors
• _____	_____
• _____	_____
• _____	_____
• _____	_____
• _____	_____
• _____	_____

2. Look at the diagram of an elevator.

a. The upward movement of the elevator is

   linked to the _____ movement
   <small>upward / downward</small>

   of a counterweight.

b. Mr. Winter is on the third floor. If he wants to go to the ground floor, how must the counterweight move?

   _____

An Elevator

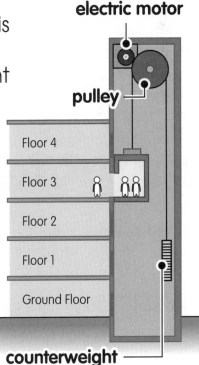

electric motor

pulley

Floor 4

Floor 3

Floor 2

Floor 1

Ground Floor

counterweight

ISBN: 978-1-897457-76-4

6 Pulley Power

A single pulley can help us lift and lower loads by changing the direction of our force. We can also connect pulleys in order to use less force to lift a load. In this unit, you will see how pulley systems divide the weight of a load, and how the number of pulleys in a system can affect the force required to lift a load.

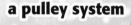
a pulley system

After completing this unit, you will

- understand the difference between a single pulley and a pulley system.
- know what a movable pulley is.
- understand the advantages of pulley systems.

We have to say "thank you" to the pulley system; without it, we would have a hard time getting to the top of the hill.

fixed pulley

movable pulley

Vocabulary

fixed pulley: a pulley attached to a fixed structure above the load being lifted

movable pulley: a pulley attached to the load being lifted

ISBN: 978-1-897457-76-4

Pulleys are widely used, from window blinds in our houses to cranes on construction sites. Did you know that we also use pulleys in hospitals to help patients with broken bones?

A pulley system helps stretch the tight muscles around a broken bone but keeps the broken bone in place so that it will heal properly.

Pulleys are used in hospitals, too.

A. Write a short paragraph to describe how a flagpole works.

How a Pulley Makes a
Flagpole Work

_____

_____

_____

_____

_____

_____

_____

B. Look at the experiments and the record. Answer the questions.

Force Needed to Lift a Weight		
Weight	**Experiment 1**	**Experiment 2**
100 N	100 N	50 N
200 N	200 N	100 N
360 N	360 N	180 N

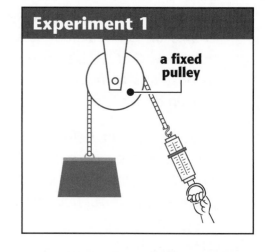

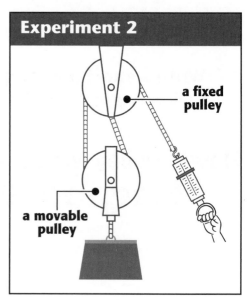

1. How much force is needed to lift a weight of 200 N

   a. with one pulley? _____

   b. with two pulleys? _____

2. Predict how much force is needed to lift a weight of 420 N

   a. with one pulley. _____

   b. with two pulleys. _____

3. A system with two pulleys requires _____ the

   none of / half

   amount of effort needed to lift a load with one pulley.

4. What happens when the number of pulleys in a system is increased?

   _____

C. Look at the experiments. Complete the records. Then answer the questions.

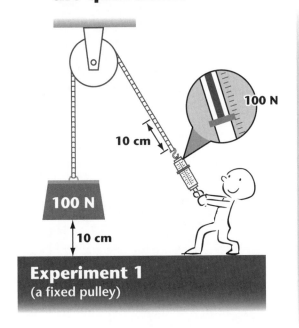

Experiment 1
(a fixed pulley)

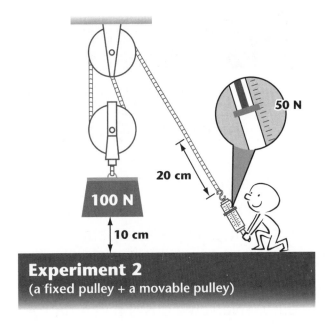

Experiment 2
(a fixed pulley + a movable pulley)

1. Lift a Weight of 100 N 10 cm High

	Force Needed	Distance Rope Is Pulled
Experiment 1		
Experiment 2		

2.

The experiments show that the force is cut in _____ when the number of
half / a second
pulleys is doubled, but the distance the rope must be pulled has _____ .
tripled / doubled

3. How does the distance over which the force is exerted change when the number of pulleys in a system is increased?

_____

D. Read the passage. Then answer the questions.

Pulleys
and the Canal Ring Houses in Amsterdam

In Amsterdam, a canal city in Europe, pulleys adorn the tops of many houses. Houses built along Amsterdam's many canals in the 1600s are tall and narrow to protect the possessions inside them from flooding. Narrow houses mean narrow doorways and narrow, steep staircases, which mean that large items cannot be moved easily within a house. Then how do people move their belongings from one floor to another? With pulleys! At the top of all of these houses is a hoist beam. A pulley is either attached to this beam, or the hoist beam leads to a pulley system in the attic. This way, furniture can be moved from floor to floor outside the house. To ensure that bigger items do not hit the exterior walls while being lifted or lowered, many houses are built tilted outwards to provide space between the house and the item.

   ISBN: 978-1-897457-76-4

1. Check the building that might be found in Amsterdam.

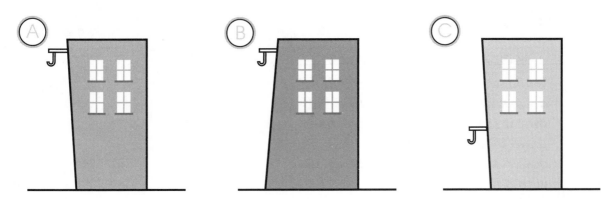

2. Draw pictures to show how a couch is moved to the second floor.

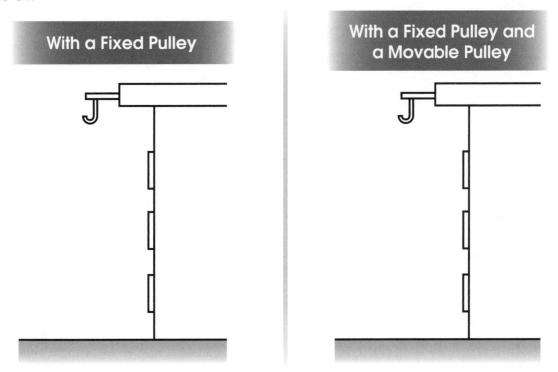

With a Fixed Pulley

With a Fixed Pulley and a Movable Pulley

3. If the couch weighs 1000 N, how much force is needed to lift it

   a. with a fixed pulley? _____

   b. with a fixed pulley and a
      movable pulley? _____

 **Experiment**

Introduction

fixed pulley

> When we lift things up by pulling down using a fixed pulley, we find that it is much easier to pull down than to pull up. Then will it be easier to lift things by pulling up with a movable pulley?

Hypothesis

It is easier to lift things with a movable pulley than with just your arm.

Materials

- *a broom*
- *two chairs*
- *a pencil*
- *a small, empty spool*
- *a wire hanger*
- *two books of equal weight*
- *a ball of twine*

Steps

1. Put the pencil through the spool. Tie some twine around one book and attach it firmly to the pencil as shown.

2. Tie some twine around the other book in the same way. Set aside.

3. Make a diamond with the wire hanger.

ISBN: 978-1-897457-76-4

4. Set up the broom and chairs as shown. Hang the hanger on the broom.

5. Tie some twine to the hanger. Loop the other end of the piece of twine around the spool.

6. Pull the free end of the twine to lift the book with one hand.

7. With your other hand, lift the second book.

Result

Which method of lifting made it easier to lift the book?

Ⓐ with the movable pulley

Ⓑ with just your arm

Conclusion

The hypothesis was: _____

_____

My experiment _____ the
hypothesis.   supported / did not support

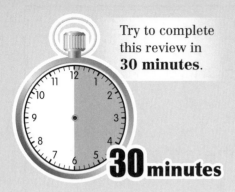

Try to complete this review in **30 minutes**.

30minutes

This review consists of five sections, from A to E. The marks for each question are shown in parentheses. The circle at the bottom right corner is for the marks you get in each section. An overall record is on the last page of the review.

A. Write T for true and F for false.

1. A gear is a wheel with teeth. **(2)** _____

2. A wheelbarrow is an example of a lever. **(2)** _____

3. The gears turn at the same speed and in opposite directions. **(2)**

   8 teeth   **16** teeth

   _____

4. Inclined planes are slanting surfaces connecting a lower level to a higher level. **(2)**

   _____

8

ISBN: 978-1-897457-76-4

B. Do the matching.

1.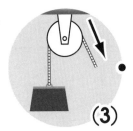
   (3) •

2.
   (3) •

3.
   (3) •

4.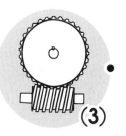
   (3) •

5.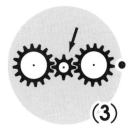
   (3) •

- • an idler gear; keeps the two connected gears rotating in the same direction

- • a rack and pinion system; a single gear meshing with a sliding toothed rack

- • a compound machine with a lever, gears, and a wheel and axle

- • a combination of a circular gear and a worm gear

- • a pulley; the load goes up when the free end of the rope is pulled down

15

 ISBN: 978-1-897457-76-4

C. Answer the questions.

1. What is a fixed pulley? **(4)**

   _____

2. What is a movable pulley? **(4)**

   _____

3. Write two rules that we should follow when we work with machines. **(8)**

   _____

   _____

   _____

4.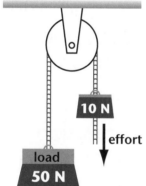

   How much more effort is needed to lift the load in this picture? **(5)**

   _____

   _____

5.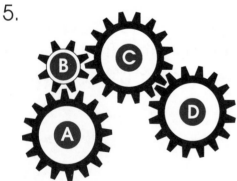

   If gear C turns clockwise, in what directions will the other gears turn? **(6)**

   _____

   _____

ISBN: 978-1-897457-76-4

D. Draw a diagram to match the descriptions. Then answer the questions.

A Gear Train with Three Gears

- Three gears are placed in a row.
- When the biggest gear turns once, the smallest gear turns twice.
- The medium-sized gear turns in a clockwise direction, which is opposite to the other two gears.

1.

A Gear Train

(16)

2. If the biggest gear has 20 teeth, how many teeth does the smallest gear have? (**2**)

   (A) 40 teeth   (B) 20 teeth   (C) 10 teeth

3. Which gear rotates the fastest? (**2**)

   (A) the largest gear

   (B) the medium-sized gear

   (C) the smallest gear

20

E. **Draw diagrams to show how to lift a book with the supplies provided in each group and draw arrows to show the movement. Then answer the questions.**

1. ━━━━━━━━━━━━━━ **Lifting a Book with Pulleys** ━━━━━━━━━━━━━━

   - a fixed pulley   • a hook   • a fixed pulley   • a hook   • a rope
   - a rope   • a book   • a movable pulley   • a book

   Design A   **Design B**

   (18)

2. How much force is needed to lift a 20 N load with

   a. design A? (**3**)   _____ N

   b. design B? (**3**)   _____ N

3. Which design cannot reduce the force needed to lift the book? Do you think it still helps make our work easier? Explain. (**6**)

   _____

   _____

   _____

   30

ISBN: 978-1-897457-76-4

My Record

Section A	8
Section B	15
Section C	27
Section D	20
Section E	30

Total

100

80-100

Great work! You really understand your science stuff! Research your favourite science topics at the library or on the Internet to find out more about the topics related to this section. Keep challenging yourself to learn more!

60-79

Good work! You understand some basic concepts, but try reading through the units again to see whether you can master the material! Go over the questions that you had trouble with to make sure you know the correct answers.

below 60

You can do much better! Try reading over the units again. Ask your parents or teachers any questions you might have. Once you feel confident that you know the material, try the review again. Science is exciting, so don't give up!

ISBN: 978-1-897457-76-4

The Biomedical Engineer

A biomedical engineer develops mechanisms that doctors use to diagnose and treat patients. One such mechanism, the cardiac pacemaker, is a battery-powered electrical device implanted inside a patient's chest to keep his or her heartbeats regular. It works by providing an electrical stimulus to the heart muscle that makes it beat without causing damage. The man who invented it, a Canadian named John A. Hopps, is considered the father of biomedical engineering.

Hopps invented the first cardiac pacemaker in 1950 with surgeons Dr. W.G. Bigelow and Dr. John Callaghan. Unlike modern pacemakers, it was far too large to be implanted into a patient's body and was powered by an electrical outlet, not batteries. It was not until 1957 that a Swedish team developed a pacemaker small enough to fit into a patient's chest.

Hopps led the development of many medical devices over the length of his career, helping people with many types of disabilities. In 1984, Hopps benefited directly from his invention, when he needed and received a cardiac pacemaker.

ISBN: 978-1-897457-76-4

ISBN: 978-1-897457-76-4

1 What simple machine can be found in a zipper?

2 Which simple machines make up a gear?

Output

- screw
- pulley
- wedge
- wheel and axle
- lever
- inclined plane

3 Which simple machines are not used to transport objects?

4 Are gears always circles?

5 What was the first use of the wheel?

Find the answers on the next page.

Cool Science Facts

1 Wedges can be found in a zipper. A zipper has two rows of teeth that fit together to make a tight seam. A slider is used to push the teeth together or pull them apart. The slider itself has a wedge shape and there are three more wedges inside the slider working together to make a zipper work. When you pull the slider up, two wedges on the sides push the teeth together.

2 A gear is a wheel and axle, except that the wheel has teeth so that it can work together with other gears.

slider

teeth

This wedge forces the teeth apart when you undo the zipper.

These two wedges push the teeth together when you zip up.

axle

wheel

ISBN: 978-1-897457-76-4

4

Gears are not always circles. They can come in many shapes, including squares, triangles, and rectangles.

These shapes are used for different purposes, like changing the direction of the movement.

worm gear

5

Archaeological excavations have shown that people used a potter's wheel in Mesopotamia as early as 3500 BCE, which was about 5500 years ago.

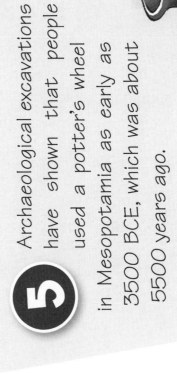

3

The wedge is designed to separate objects, while the screw attaches objects together.

wedge

screw

ISBN: 978-1-897457-76-4

ISBN: 978-1-897457-76-4

Section 3

Understanding Matter and Energy

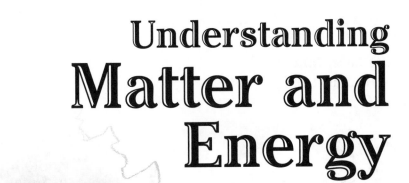

ISBN: 978-1-897457-76-4

1 Light around Us

Light is a form of energy that is all around us. In this unit, you will see that there are natural and artificial light sources and that some objects emit light while others reflect it. You will also see that light travels in straight lines.

*The sun **emits** light, and my sunglasses **reflect** it.*

After completing this unit, you will

- know that light sources can be natural or artificial.
- know that some objects emit light and others reflect it.
- know that light travels in straight lines.

Vocabulary

natural light: light produced by the sun or by nature

artificial light: light produced by humans; does not occur naturally

emit: give off (light)

reflect: throw back (light) from a surface

artificial light

ISBN: 978-1-897457-76-4

Light is all around you, but you cannot hear or feel it. You become aware of it when it reaches your eyes. Without light, you cannot see anything at all! The sun is our main source of light. Its light is very strong and it can reach us even when it is very cloudy. It is so strong that we should never look directly at it, as it could damage our eyes.

Don't look directly at the sun, Teddy.

A. Fill in the blanks. Then sort the pictures of light sources and give one example for each.

A

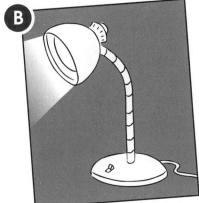

B

Light Sources   natural   artificial

- Light that occurs in nature is

  _____ light.

  e.g. ◯ ; _____

- Light that is created by people, and does not occur naturally, is

  _____ light.

  e.g. ◯ ; _____

ISBN: 978-1-897457-76-4

B. **Fill in the blanks with the words "emit" or "reflect". Then sort the objects and answer the question.**

What Emits or Reflects Light?

Most things, such as rocks, pencils, and mirrors, do not 1._____ their own light; we see them because light bounces off them. They 2._____ light. Some things reflect light better than others. Things that 3._____ light are our light sources.

bounce off (reflect)

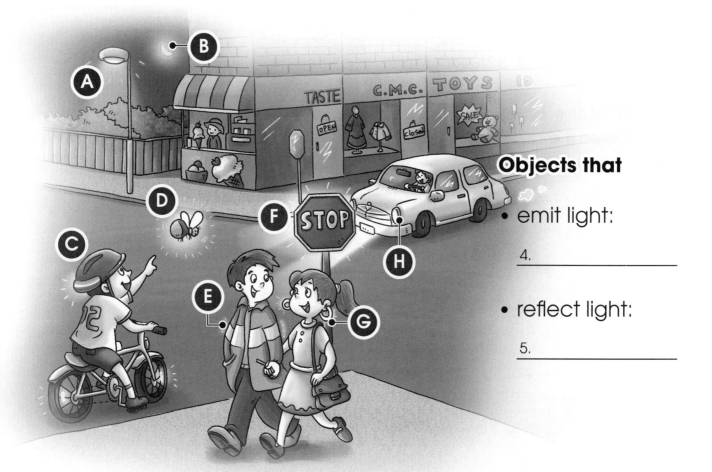

Objects that

- emit light:

  4._____

- reflect light:

  5._____

6. Which objects shown in the picture are safety reflectors? How do they keep people safe?

_____

_____

 ISBN: 978-1-897457-76-4

C. Fill in the blanks with the given words. Then check the correct picture in each pair to show how light travels.

reflected   straight   direction

Light travels in 1._____ lines. It always travels like this unless it meets something that makes it change 2._____ . Once the light hits an object and it changes its direction, we can see the object because the light is 3._____ into our eyes. Since light has this property, we are not able to see around a bend in the road.

4.

5.

6.

2 Light: Reflection and Refraction

We see because of light. In this unit, you will learn about two special properties of light – reflection and refraction – and recognize that reflection and refraction are important in our daily lives.

After completing this unit, you will

- know what reflection and refraction of light are.
- understand why we see a rainbow.
- understand how we see colours.

> *The refraction of light makes his eye look so big!*

vocabulary

reflection: happens when light bounces off an object instead of being soaked up

refraction: happens when light bends or changes its angle as it passes from one material to another

absorb: take in (light)

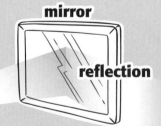

Pools, lakes, and rivers often appear less deep than they really are because water acts just like a magnifying lens, bending light to make it seem like the bottom of these bodies of water are nearer to us than they are. Next time you go swimming with your parents, try picking up an object from under the water. You might find that it is deeper than you think.

A. Fill in the blanks with "reflection" or "refraction". Then match the pictures with the correct descriptions.

Properties of Light

When light hits an object and bounces off, it creates a _____ . •

Light travels in a straight line, but when it passes through another medium such as water, it may bend and change direction. This is called _____ . •

B. Fill in the blanks with the given words. Then colour the rainbow.

red	white	direction	refraction	yellow	green
blue	indigo	violet	raindrop	orange	

Since sunlight appears to have no colours, we call it
1. _____ light, but it is really made up of all the colours of
the rainbow: 2. _____ , 3. _____ , 4. _____ ,
5. _____ , 6. _____ , 7. _____ , and
8. _____ . When white light meets a 9. _____ , it
changes 10. _____ . This change of direction is called
11. _____ . When the colours in the light are refracted
and separated, a beautiful rainbow is formed.

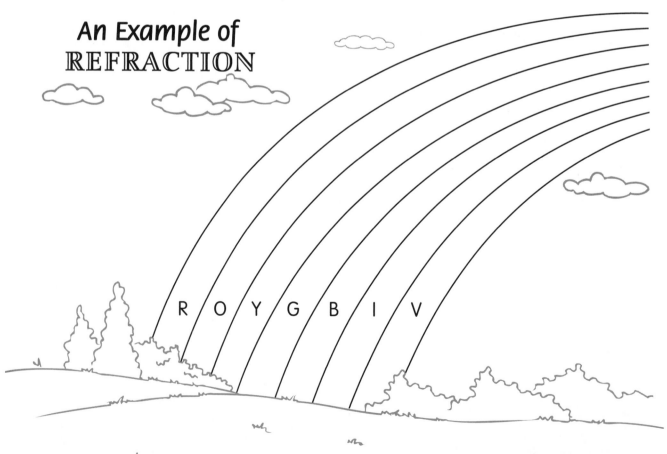

An Example of REFRACTION

R O Y G B I V

ISBN: 978-1-897457-76-4

C. Fill in the blanks to complete the descriptions. Then answer the question.

How Do We See Colours?

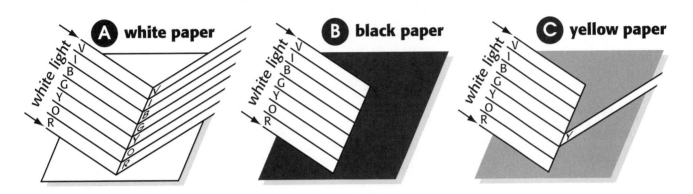

A When sunlight shines on a white surface, we see

_____ because the surface _____ all the
   white/black   reflects/absorbs

colours.

B When sunlight shines on a black surface, we see

_____ because all the colours have been
   white/black

taken in or _____ .
            reflected/absorbed

C When sunlight shines on a yellow surface, we see

_____ because all the colours except yellow
   yellow/red

have been _____ by the surface.
          reflected/absorbed

What makes a green frog green?

_____

_____

3 Light: Transparency

Light can pass through some materials but not others. In this unit, you will see what some of these materials are. You will also see how shadows are formed.

After completing this unit, you will

- know the difference between transparent, translucent, and opaque materials and understand why they are used.

- understand how a shadow is formed.

The box is opaque, so you cannot see what I bought you.

v o c a b u l a r y

transparent

transparent: allowing light to pass through easily, so objects can be seen clearly

translucent: allowing only some light to pass through, so objects cannot be seen clearly

opaque: allowing no light to pass through, so objects cannot be seen

ISBN: 978-1-897457-76-4

Have you ever seen your shadow? When you stand outdoors in the sunlight, light cannot pass through your body. Some light is reflected and some is absorbed by your body. Therefore, there is an area on the ground that light does not reach. This is your shadow.

The size of your shadow is not fixed. Do you know how to make it shrink or grow?

A. Colour each rectangle with the specified colour. Then fill in the blanks.

opaque   transparent   translucent

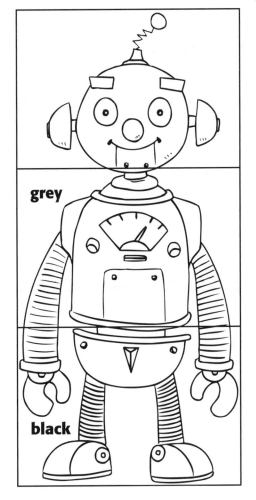

1.

_____ material:

• Light passes through it, allowing objects to be seen clearly.

2.

grey

_____ material:

• Some light passes through it, causing objects to be seen less clearly.

3.

black

_____ material:

• No light passes through it, preventing objects from being seen.

B. Identify the material each object is made of and decide which type of material each person needs.

Material

Transparent •

Translucent •

Opaque •

• Sam does not want people to touch his sculpture, but he wants them to be able to see it.

• Emma does not want her father to see the gift she has made him.

• Sasha wants a window on her door, but she still wants to have some privacy.

C. Write a situation when it would be best to use each type of material.

transparent: _____

translucent: _____

opaque: _____

ISBN: 978-1-897457-76-4

D. Fill in the blanks with the given words. Then check the correct shadows and cross out the incorrect one.

straight   opaque   length   shadow

Light travels in 1._____ lines. When light cannot pass through an object, the object casts a 2._____ . Therefore, 3._____ objects cast shadows. The 4._____ , size, and position of a shadow depend on where the light is coming from in relation to an object.

> *The nearer the object is to the flashlight, the larger its shadow.*

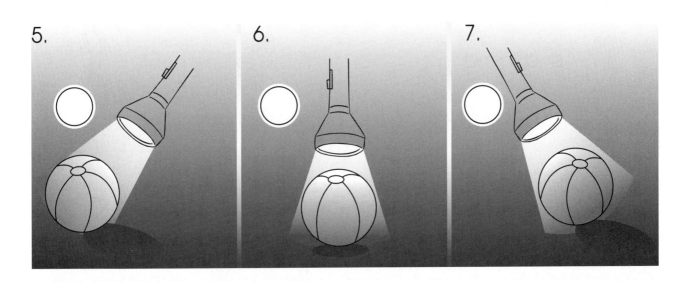

5.　　　　　　　　　6.　　　　　　　　　7.

Experiment

Introduction

When the sun rises in the morning, it lights up most of what I can see. When light is everywhere, how can I know for sure that it travels in straight lines?

Hypothesis

Light travels in straight lines.

Materials

- *a cereal box*
- *scissors*
- *a one-hole punch*
- *a dark room*
- *3 thick, heavy books*
- *a flashlight*

Steps

1. Ask a friend to help you with this experiment.

2. Cut out the two "faces" of a cereal box.

3. Holding them together, punch a hole close to the top side of the faces.

          ISBN: 978-1-897457-76-4

4. Lay the three books in a row on a table. Wedge each cereal box face between the books as shown in the picture. Align the holes.

5. Turn out the lights. Look through the hole while your friend shines the flashlight through his or hers.

6. Rotate your cereal box face so that the holes are no longer aligned. Repeat step 5.

Result

Could you see the flashlight's light when the holes:

• were aligned? _____

• were not aligned? _____

Conclusion

The hypothesis was: _____

_____

My experiment _____ the hypothesis.
                    supported / did not support

ISBN: 978-1-897457-76-4

4 What Is Sound?

A sound is made when something vibrates. In this unit, you will learn how vibrations cause sounds and how sounds travel. You will also learn about how a sound's pitch is related to vibration.

After completing this unit, you will

- know what sound is.
- know how sound travels.
- know what pitch is.

Teddy, don't tell Alex that I got him a robot for Christmas.

A robot!

ROBOT

Vocabulary

vibration: a quick, back-and-forth motion

pitch: the lowness or highness of a sound

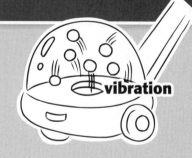

vibration

   ISBN: 978-1-897457-76-4

In different environments, we can hear different sounds. Go to some different places and make a chart to record the sounds that you hear. Then describe the loudness of the sounds and write about how the sounds make you feel. Do some sounds make you feel nervous, energetic, calm, or happy?

Stadium – sounds that I can hear
1. **screaming**: loud, makes me excited
2. **clapping**: not loud, makes me happy

A. Look at the pictures. Then fill in the blanks with the given words.

vibrates
vibrate
sound
vibrating

The Cause of Sound: Vibration

Hold one end of a ruler and pluck the other end with your finger.

The ruler 1._____ and makes the air around it 2._____ too.

The 3._____ air carries the 4._____ to the ear.

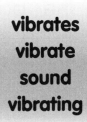

The greater the vibration is, the louder the sound.

B. Try the experiments to see whether or not sound travels through different media. Circle the correct word and answer the questions.

Sound travels through...

Experiment 1: Air (Materials: two spoons)

Bang two spoons together.

Can you hear the sounds of the spoons clinking? _____

Conclusion: Sound **can / cannot** travel through air.

Experiment 2: Water (Materials: a balloon and water)

Fill the balloon with water. Listen while someone speaks with their lips against the balloon.

Can the listener hear the speaker? _____

Conclusion: _____

Experiment 3: Solid

(Materials: two yogurt cups and a piece of string)

Poke a hole in the bottom of each cup. Thread the ends of a piece of string through the holes. Pull the string tight and tie a knot inside each cup.

Can your friend hear what you say when you speak into the cup? _____

Conclusion: _____

ISBN: 978-1-897457-76-4

C. Read the paragraph. Describe the sounds that the children make with the given words. Give examples of high- and low-pitched sounds.

If an object vibrates quickly, it makes a high-pitched sound. When you blow a whistle, the air inside vibrates quickly, and it makes a high-pitched sound. However, if an object vibrates slowly, it makes a low-pitched sound. When a drummer hits the skin of a big drum, the skin vibrates slowly. This makes a low-pitched sound. Some things vibrate so fast or so slow that humans cannot even hear the sounds they make.

fast   slow
high   low

1. Vibration: _____slow_____

   Pitch: _____

2. Sound could be from:

   examples
   • **drum**

   • _____

3. Vibration: _____

   Pitch: _____

4. Sound could be from:

   examples
   • **whistle**

   • _____

5 What Happens to Sound

Sounds can be modified, reflected, or absorbed. In this unit, you will learn about how a sound's loudness is measured, and about how sound is reflected, absorbed, and modified. You will also learn about how a human ear works.

barrier

*This barrier along the highway can **absorb** sounds.*

After completing this unit, you will

- know that sound can be measured in decibels.
- understand how sound is modified, reflected, and absorbed.
- understand how the human ear works.

Vocabulary

echo: sound reflecting

modify: change

reflect: bounce back or off, like a sound wave bouncing off a wall as an echo

absorb: take in, like a carpet absorbing sounds in a living room

Have you ever noticed that the engine sounds of a rumbling truck become louder as the truck gets closer to you? Do you know why this happens?

Sound is caused by vibrations, and vibrations in air become weaker and weaker as they travel; therefore, sound is quieter far away than it is close up. The closer you are to a sound, the louder it is.

Look at an airplane in the sky. Can you hear any noise from the airplane? The airplane sounds quiet to you when it is up in the sky and you are on the ground.

A. Fill in the blanks and complete the chart on the loudness of different sounds.

The 1. _____ of a sound can be measured in 2. _____ (dB).

decibels	loudness
a whisper
a jackhammer
a busy street

Sound	Loudness (dB)
airplane taking off	130
3.	110
someone shouting	100
a vacuum cleaner	80
4.	70
people talking	50
a quiet street	40
5.	30
a pin dropping	10

B. Fill in the blanks to show the properties of sound. Then circle the correct answers.

Properties of Sound

absorbed   reflected   modified
pitch   loudness

1. Sound can be r_____ from a **hard / soft** surface.
    • In a good concert hall, the right amount of reflected sound blending with direct sound makes the overall sound **poorer / richer** .

    • **An echo / Thunder** is an example of reflected sound.

2. Sound can be a_____ by a **hard / soft** surface.
    • **Carpeting / Wooden flooring** absorbs the sound of footsteps.

    • Music recording studios use sound **absorbing / reflecting** materials on their walls to eliminate any unwanted sound.

3. Sound can be m_____ .

    • L_____
    The harder you hit a drum, the **softer / louder** the sound it makes.

    • P_____
    The tighter the string of an instrument is, the **higher / lower** the pitch you get.

ISBN: 978-1-897457-76-4

C. Fill in the blanks with the words from the diagram to complete the paragraph.

Sound waves are collected by the o_____ ear, which is made up of the _____ , the _____ , and the _____ , a thin-skinned structure stretched tight like a drum that vibrates with sound waves. Waves travel through the ear canal and the eardrum to the m_____ ear. The middle ear's three _____ amplify the eardrum's vibrations and send them to the i_____ ear. Here, the snail-shaped _____ changes vibrations into signals that are carried by _____ to your brain.

Cross-section of an Ear

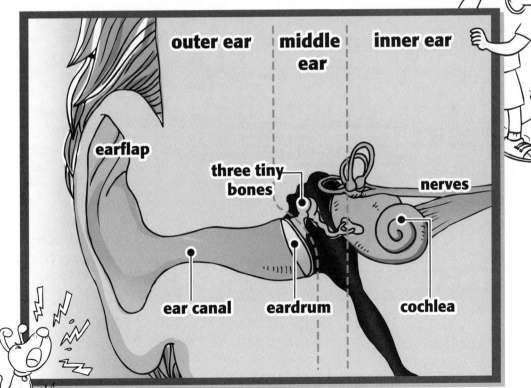

outer ear   middle ear   inner ear

earflap

three tiny bones

nerves

ear canal   eardrum   cochlea

6 How We Use Light and Sound

We use light and sound all the time in everyday life. In this unit, you will see how we protect ourselves from excessive light and sound, how everyday items make use of the properties of light and sound, and how animals use sound.

After completing this unit, you will

- know some items that protect you from excessive light and sound.
- know some items that make use of the properties of light and sound.
- know what echolocation is.

echolocation

I know where you are!

hat: protects against excessive sun

Vocabulary

excessive: too much

echolocation: using sound to orient or locate

 ISBN: 978-1-897457-76-4

Sounds can tell us a lot about the world around us. They tell us when someone is calling us (a phone ringing), when it is lunch break at school (a bell ringing), and when it is time to wake up in the morning (an alarm clock ringing). Do you have some other ideas about how sound can convey messages?

Make a chart to list them out.

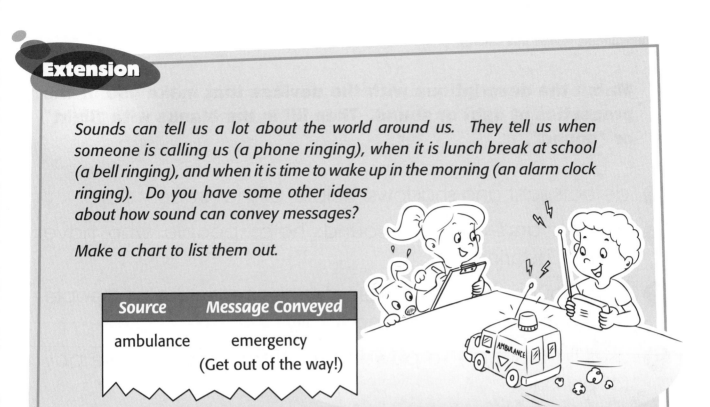

Source	Message Conveyed
ambulance	emergency (Get out of the way!)

A. Draw lines to show which items protect you from too much light or sound. Then give a reason why it is important to protect yourself from too much light or sound.

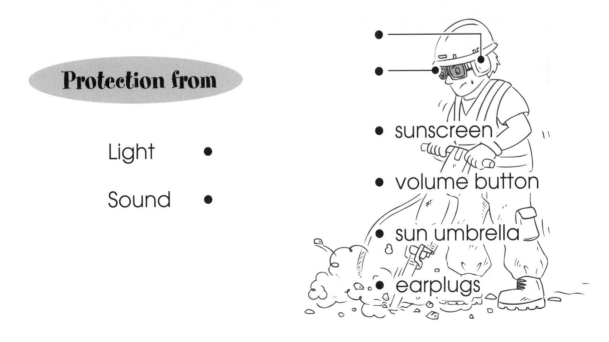

Protection from

Light •

Sound •

• sunscreen
• volume button
• sun umbrella
• earplugs

_____

_____

B. Match the descriptions with the devices that make use of the properties of light or sound. Then fill in the blanks with "light" or "sound".

A detects light and shadows; helpful at the grocery store

B gathers and amplifies sound; helps people who have trouble hearing

C turns sound waves into electrical energy; helps people talk to faraway friends and family

D uses light energy to power its battery; helps people pay for parking

E uses lenses to refract light in order to make objects appear closer; helps astronomers see the stars

F turns sound waves into electrical energy; helps an audience hear someone on a stage

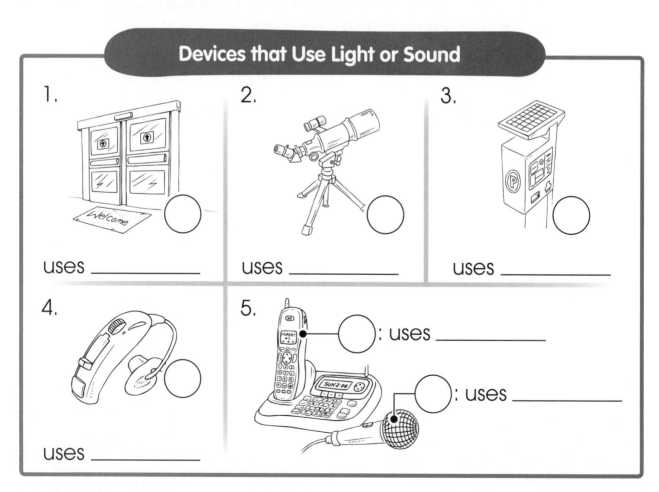

Devices that Use Light or Sound

1.
uses _____

2.
uses _____

3.
uses _____

4.
uses _____

5.
: uses _____
: uses _____

ISBN: 978-1-897457-76-4

C. Fill in the blanks with the given words to complete the paragraph.

surface	echo	water	echolocation
communicate	air	sound	whale

Like humans, animals use 1._____ to convey messages. Some bat and 2._____ species use something called 3._____ to find food, orient themselves, and 4._____ with one another. Echolocation involves an animal calling out and listening for an 5._____ – sound bouncing off a 6._____ – to know where the surface is. This way, animals can locate things like insects or fish. Bats send their calls through 7._____ , while whales send them through water. Both methods are effective, but whales have an advantage over bats: sound travels faster and farther in 8._____ than in air.

Experiment

Introduction

I hear echoes in places like the bathroom and the concert hall, but not in places like my studio or my carpeted bedroom. Do smooth surfaces, like tiled surfaces, reflect sound? Do rough surfaces, like carpeted surfaces, absorb it?

Hypothesis

Smooth surfaces reflect sound; rough surfaces absorb it.

Materials

- 2 gift wrap tubes
- a ticking cooking timer
- a stuffed toy
- a mirror

Steps

1. Put one tube on a table so that the timer is at one end and the mirror is at the other end.

2. Put the other tube on the table so that the mirror is at one end and your ear is at the other. Together, the tubes should form a wide "V".

ISBN: 978-1-897457-76-4

3. Listen for the sound of the timer through the tube and record your result.

4. Repeat steps 1 to 3, replacing the mirror with the stuffed toy.

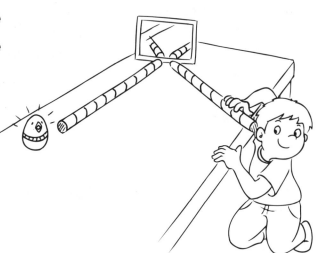

Result

Record.

Object	Surface (rough / smooth)	Echo (loud / quiet / none)
mirror		
stuffed toy		

Which material created a louder echo?

_____

Conclusion

The hypothesis was: _____

_____

My experiment _____ the
hypothesis.   supported / did not support

This review consists of five sections, from A to E. The marks for each question are shown in parentheses. The circle at the bottom right corner is for the marks you get in each section. An overall record is on the last page of the review.

A. Write T for true and F for false.

1. The loudness of a sound can be measured in decibels. (**2**) _____

2. When an object vibrates quickly, it makes a high-pitched sound. (**2**) _____

3. Echolocation involves using light to orient and locate. (**2**) _____

4. Car lights reflect light and traffic signs emit it. (**2**) _____

8

ISBN: 978-1-897457-76-4

B. Do the matching.

1.  (2)

2.  (2)

3.  (2)

4.  (2)

5.  (2)

- medium that refracts light

- protects ears from excessive sound

- artificial source of light

- makes a low-pitched sound

- natural source of light

10

C. Check the properties of light and cross out the wrong ones. Then answer the questions.

1. **Properties of Light** (**2** each)

   (A) Light travels in straight lines.

   (B) Light travels in air only.

   (C) Light can be absorbed.

   (D) Light can be reflected.

   (E) Light can be evaporated under high temperatures.

   (F) Light can be refracted.

2. Which property of light is shown in each situation?

   a. When a light shines on a black surface, we see black. (**4**)

      Property of Light: _____

   b. When you look at the front of a fish tank, the fish appear closer to you than they really are. (**4**)

      Property of Light: _____

3. What makes a red apple red? (**6**)

   _____

   _____

   _____

26

ISBN: 978-1-897457-76-4

D. Check the properties of sound and cross out the wrong ones. Then answer the questions.

1. **Properties of Sound** (**2** each)

    (A) Sound travels through air only.

    (B) Sound can be absorbed.

    (C) Sound can be reflected.

    (D) Sound travels through air, water, and solids.

    (E) The loudness of sounds can be modified, but the pitch cannot.

    (F) The pitch and loudness of sounds can be modified.

2. If you clapped your hands in the rooms described, in which room would you hear an echo? Explain your choice. (**6**)

    (A) a bathroom with mirrors and tiles

    (B) a bedroom with curtains, a bed, and a couch

    Explain: _____

3. If an elastic band is stretched and then plucked, it makes a sound.

    a. Explain how the sound is created. (**4**)

    _____

    b. If the elastic band is plucked harder, what will happen to the sound? (**4**)

    _____

    _____

26

E. Answer the questions.

1. Name and describe the function of each labelled part of the ear.

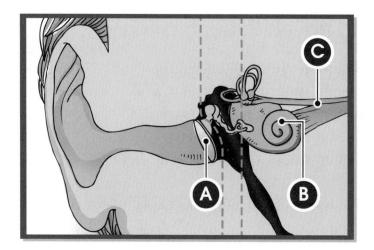

A _____ **(2)** ; _____ **(4)**

B _____ **(2)** ; _____ **(4)**

C _____ **(2)** ; _____ **(4)**

2. Name the items.

   a. an item that can protect us from excessive light
   _____ **(3)**

   b. an item that can protect us from excessive sound
   _____ **(3)**

   c. a device that helps a person who has trouble hearing
   _____ **(3)**

   d. a device that helps astronomers see the stars
   _____ **(3)**

30

ISBN: 978-1-897457-76-4

My Record

Section **A**	8
Section **B**	10
Section **C**	26
Section **D**	26
Section **E**	30

Total

100

80-100

Great work! You really understand your science stuff! Research your favourite science topics at the library or on the Internet to find out more about the topics related to this section. Keep challenging yourself to learn more!

60-79

Good work! You understand some basic concepts, but try reading through the units again to see whether you can master the material! Go over the questions that you had trouble with to make sure you know the correct answers.

below 60

You can do much better! Try reading over the units again. Ask your parents or teachers any questions you might have. Once you feel confident that you know the material, try the review again. Science is exciting, so don't give up!

ISBN: 978-1-897457-76-4

Scientists at Work

The Ophthalmologist

Eyes are the organs that allow us to see things. Like our other body parts, our eyes are the specialty of a special group of doctors who dedicate themselves to understanding and treating them. These doctors are called ophthalmologists.

Fred Hollows was an ophthalmologist born in New Zealand in 1929. He worked in rural communities in New Zealand and Australia, as well as in developing countries such as Vietnam, Nepal, and Eritrea, to help restore sight to thousands of people with trachoma, an infectious and blinding eye disease. Shortly before he died in 1993, Hollows set up The Fred Hollows Foundation. Its goal is to give people in developing countries access to eye care, surgery, and affordable eyeglasses. It has been said that over one million people are able to see because of Fred Hollows's work and his Foundation.

ISBN: 978-1-897457-76-4

Cool Science Facts

1 Do animals hear the same things we hear?

2 What can you hear in space?

Is someone singing?

3 Can we use sound to clean things?

4 Why do we see lightning before we hear thunder?

5 Which is hotter – lightning or the surface of the sun?

Find the answers on the next page.

ISBN: 978-1-897457-76-4

2 Sounds are vibrations through air particles, but there is no air in space. Therefore, there is no sound in space.

Cool Science Facts

1 Animals have different ranges of hearing. Some animals, like bats and dolphins, emit and hear high pitch sounds that we cannot normally hear. They use these sounds to communicate and to find food through echolocation. Even some pets, like dogs, have a wider range of hearing than humans. They have a stronger sense of hearing than we do.

ISBN: 978-1-897457-76-4

3

We can use high frequency (high pitch) sounds of 150 kHz to 400 kHz to clean objects like electronics, jewellery, and hospital equipment. The high pitch removes dirt because of its very fast vibration.

4

Thunder is the sound that lightning makes. We see lightning first because light travels faster than sound. The speed of light is about 300 000 000 m/s, while the speed of sound is only about 340 m/s.

5

Although the surface of the sun is extremely hot at 5500°C, lightning can get as hot as 28 000°C! We feel heat from the sun but not from lightning because the sun is so much bigger.

ISBN: 978-1-897457-76-4

ISBN: 978-1-897457-76-4

Section **4**

Understanding
Earth and Space
Systems

ISBN: 978-1-897457-76-4

1 Rocks and Minerals

Rocks build the land around us, and minerals make up the rocks. In this unit, you will see that rocks form much of our landscape. You will learn about some of the characteristics of rocks and learn about geology.

Mom, I think rocks are like cookies, and minerals are like the ingredients.

After completing this unit, you will

- know the difference between rocks and minerals.
- know some of the characteristics of rocks and minerals.
- know what geology is.

"rocks"

"minerals"

ROCKY COOKIES

FLOUR

CREAM

BUTTER

diamond – a mineral

Vocabulary

mineral: a natural, solid, inorganic material with a specific chemical make-up and a crystal structure

rock: a natural, solid, inorganic material made of one or more minerals

geology: the study of the earth

inorganic: not living

Have you seen the stone landmarks built by the Inuit, the indigenous people of the Arctic region? These landmark structures, called inukshuks, have been used for navigation or as a point of reference for many years. They are either a single stone positioned in an upright manner or many rocks piled high in the shape of a human figure. Since rocks are strong materials, these structures stay upright for years.

You can collect some rocks in your backyard and balance them to build your own inukshuk. Then explore different ways in which you can make your structure balance.

inukshuk

A. **Check all the places where you can find rocks. Then give one example of your own.**

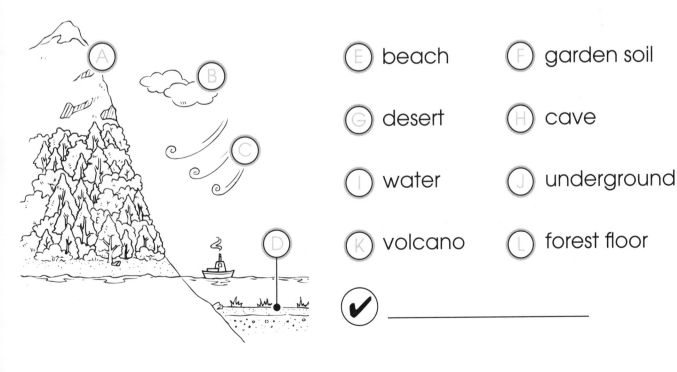

(E) beach   (F) garden soil

(G) desert   (H) cave

(I) water   (J) underground

(K) volcano   (L) forest floor

(✔) _____

B. **Complete the descriptions with the given words. Then answer the questions.**

Type	Characteristic		Example
mineral	crystal	inorganic	
rock	natural	minerals	diamond sandstone

1. **Type:** _____

   - solid, natural, _____
   - specific chemical make-up
   - a _____ structure
   - e.g. _____

   Type: _____

   - solid, _____ , inorganic
   - made up of one or more _____
   - e.g. _____

2. What makes rocks and minerals similar?

   _____

3. What makes them different?

   _____

4. Identify each as a rock or a mineral.

_____   _____   _____

ISBN: 978-1-897457-76-4

C. Read the paragraph. Then fill out the geology fact card.

Geology is the study of the earth. Many geologists study rocks and minerals, as rocks and minerals are some of the best clues to understanding what happened on Earth in the past, what is happening now, and what will happen. Rocks and minerals can tell geologists about everything from land movement billions of years ago, to what is at the centre of the Earth, to where earthquakes are likely to happen and when volcanoes are likely to erupt.

Geology Fact Card	
Geology is: 1._____ _____ _____ Things that many geologists study: 2._____ _____	Things that rocks and minerals can tell us about: • 3._____ • 4._____ • 5._____ • 6._____

2 Minerals

Geologists find ways to classify thousands of minerals on Earth. In this unit, you will learn about how to classify minerals by their properties and test the properties of minerals.

After completing this unit, you will

- know the properties that are used to identify minerals.
- know some tests used to identify the physical properties of minerals.

I can't see how many gold coins there are because they are opaque, but I can see that they are shiny!

Vocabulary

lustre: the way that light reflects off the surface of a mineral

transparency: how well light can pass through a mineral

hardness: how difficult it is to scratch a mineral

streak: the colour of a mineral's powder

lustre: glassy

ISBN: 978-1-897457-76-4

Minerals are not just buried deep in rocks; they can be found around your house! In the kitchen, you might find table salt (mineral: halite), aluminum foil (mineral: aluminum), and copper pots (mineral: copper). In your pencil case, you might find pencil cores made of a mineral called graphite. Check to see what minerals you might find in your house.

A. Write the properties that we can use to identify minerals and the words we use to describe them.

Properties of Minerals

lustre
colour
streak
hardness
transparency

dull   soft
translucent

1. _____ : how well light can pass through a mineral; e.g. opaque, _____ , and transparent

2. _____ : the way that light reflects off a mineral's surface; e.g. metallic, glassy, waxy, and _____

3. _____ : a mineral's colour; e.g. colour names

4. _____ : how difficult it is to scratch a mineral; e.g. hard and _____

5. _____ : the colour of a mineral's powder; e.g. colour names

B. What properties of minerals do the tests reveal? Write the answers on the lines. Then match the mineral samples with their descriptions and circle the correct words.

Test 1 Scratching a mineral with another mineral

Property Revealed: 1._____

Test 2 Rubbing a mineral on a rough surface to see if it leaves a streak

Property Revealed: 2._____

Test 3 Observing how light interacts with a mineral

Properties Revealed: 3._____

4. _____
mineral
- green
- leaves a bluish streak
- **metallic / waxy**
- **opaque / transparent**

Mineral Samples

turquoise

gold

quartz

5. _____
mineral
- yellow
- leaves a yellow streak
- **metallic / glassy**
- **translucent / opaque**

6. _____
mineral
- colourless
- leaves a white streak
- **glassy / dull**
- **translucent / opaque**

ISBN: 978-1-897457-76-4

C. Read the paragraph. Then complete the Mohs Scale of Hardness and answer the questions.

The Mohs Scale of Hardness lists certain minerals from 1 to 10, with 1 being the softest and 10 being the hardest. A mineral has the ability to scratch another mineral that is softer, but not one that is harder. Every mineral is given a hardness number based on its ability to scratch and be scratched.

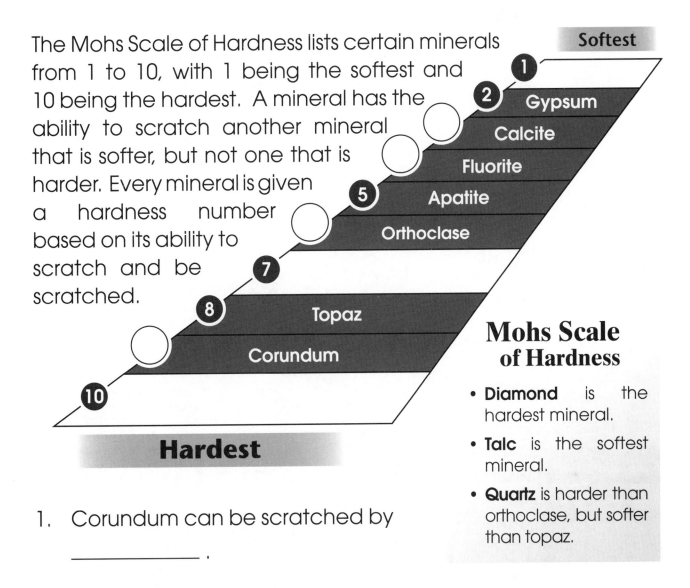

Softest

1
2 Gypsum
Calcite
Fluorite
5 Apatite
Orthoclase

7
8 Topaz
Corundum
10

Hardest

Mohs Scale of Hardness

- **Diamond** is the hardest mineral.
- **Talc** is the softest mineral.
- **Quartz** is harder than orthoclase, but softer than topaz.

1. Corundum can be scratched by _____ .

2. Your fingernail has a hardness of 2.5 and can scratch _____ and _____ .

Never test good mineral samples or anything of high value, such as jewellery, because the damage caused by a scratch could be permanent.

3. Name two minerals that can be scratched by a mineral with a hardness of 6.5.

_____

3 Rocks

There are many different kinds of rocks around you. They are made of different materials and were formed in different ways. In this unit, you will learn about the three main types of rocks: igneous, sedimentary, and metamorphic.

After completing this unit, you will

- understand that rocks have unique characteristics that are a result of how they were formed.
- know the characteristics of the three classes of rocks.

PROJECT: MAKING A SEDIMENTARY ROCK

layers of sediment

Modelling Clay

Vocabulary

magma: liquid rock underground

lava: liquid rock above ground

fossil: trace of a living thing in rock

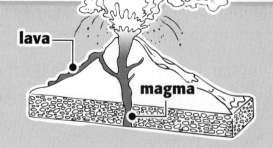

lava

magma

ISBN: 978-1-897457-76-4

You can walk around your community and collect different rock samples. An egg carton is a great place to store your rocks, but first, use an old toothbrush and some water to clean each rock sample. Then observe the colours and lustre of the rocks, make streaks, and feel their textures. Number the rocks and record their information.

Found: park
Colour: brownish grey
Lustre: dull
Streak: grey
Texture: rough

A. Match each rock type with its materials.

Types of Rocks

igneous

sedimentary

metamorphic

Materials

• igneous or sedimentary rocks

• sediment – pebbles, sand, mud

• magma (liquid rock beneath the earth) or lava (liquid rock that comes to the earth's surface)

ISBN: 978-1-897457-76-4

B. Identify the different types of rocks. Fill in the blanks with the given words and write the examples.

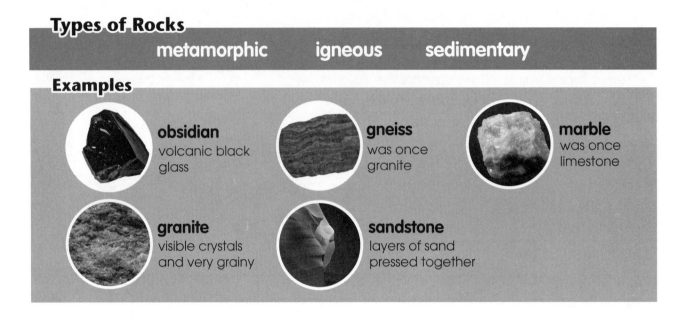

Types of Rocks

metamorphic   igneous   sedimentary

Examples

obsidian
volcanic black glass

gneiss
was once granite

marble
was once limestone

granite
visible crystals and very grainy

sandstone
layers of sand pressed together

Types of Rocks

1. [_____] rock

lava	magma
small	cools

a. **intrusive**

- formed when _____ cools and hardens below the earth's surface

- magma _____ slowly, so rocks have a shiny, grainy texture and form large mineral crystals

- e.g. _____

b. **extrusive**

- formed when _____ cools and hardens on the earth's surface

- lava cools quickly, so rocks have _____ crystals or no crystals

- e.g. _____

2. [_____ rock]

under   fossils   layers

- formed when pressure from _____ of sediment presses the layers below together and dissolved minerals in water cement layers together

- often formed _____ water

- most rocks have layers, and some have _____

- e.g. _____

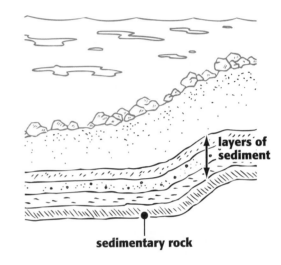

layers of sediment

sedimentary rock

3. [_____ rock]

rarely   extreme

- formed when rock is transformed into another kind of rock by _____ temperatures and pressure below the earth's surface

- these rocks _____ have fossils because the heat needed to transform rock would destroy them

- e.g.   granite (igneous rock)   limestone (sedimentary rock)

heat and pressure

heat and pressure

_____   _____

Introduction

> *Different rocks have different looks and feels, and they are made of different minerals. Do things in the environment, such as acid rain, affect different rocks differently?*

Some rocks react with vinegar – an acid like acid rain – and some do not.

Materials

- *5 to 10 different rock samples*
- *an egg carton*
- *a cup*
- *a spoon*
- *vinegar*

Steps

1. Put the 5 to 10 different rock samples in an egg carton and number them.

2. Place a rock sample in the cup and pour enough vinegar in the cup to cover the sample.

 **Rock Information**

Limestone	Granite	Quartz	Chalk
• usually white/grey	• very grainy texture	• white/pink	• soft and white
• milky looking	• often has crystals in it	• translucent	• opaque

ISBN: 978-1-897457-76-4

There are some bubbles.

3. Leave the rock for a few minutes. Observe and record what happens. Remove the rock from the cup with the spoon.

4. Repeat steps 2 and 3 with each rock sample.

5. Record.

Rock Sample	1	2	
Reaction (✔/✗)			

Result

1. Did all, some, or none of the rocks react with the vinegar?

_____

Conclusion

The hypothesis was: _____

_____

My experiment _____ the
hypothesis.
                supported / did not support

ISBN: 978-1-897457-76-4

4 The Rock Cycle

Together, igneous, sedimentary, and metamorphic rocks form a cycle. In this unit, you will learn about the rock cycle. You will see how processes like melting, extreme heat and pressure, and erosion act on rocks to transform them.

Igneous Rock

HEAT PRESSURE
HIGH   HIGH

ROCK
CYCLE

Metamorphic Rock

After completing this unit, you will

- know what erosion is.
- understand how the rock cycle happens.
- know some examples of rock transformations.

Vocabulary

erosion: the breaking off, breaking down, and moving of rock due to natural forces or human activity

extreme: intense

pressure: being pressed

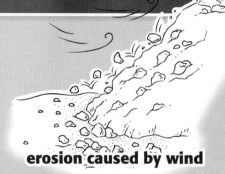

erosion caused by wind

ISBN: 978-1-897457-76-4

When you visit a beach, pick up some pebbles and check their size, shape, and texture. Take a close-up picture of each of them. Then compare them with pebbles you find in your backyard or around your neighbourhood.

You may find that the edges of the beach pebbles are rounder and smoother than the pebbles in your neighbourhood. Do you know what causes the beach pebbles to become round and smooth?

A. Fill in the blanks with the given words.

| erosion | sand | mountains | sedimentary |
| cycle | moving water |

Erosion

Pebbles, 1._____ , clay, and silt come from larger rocks,

which can come from landforms like 2._____ . Glaciers,

landslides, 3._____ , and plant roots break off or break

down rocks, causing 4._____ . All three types of

rocks can be eroded into small pieces and

eventually settle into the sea to become

5._____ rocks. Erosion

destroys rocks, and is an important

part of the rock 6._____ .

B. **Look at the rock cycle diagram. Fill in the blanks and answer the questions.**

The Rock Cycle

1. Igneous and _____ rocks can become _____ rocks under intense heat and pressure.

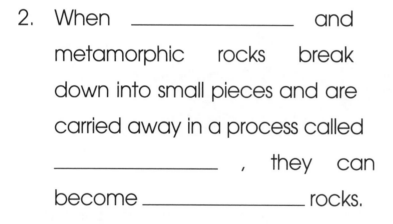

2. When _____ and metamorphic rocks break down into small pieces and are carried away in a process called _____ , they can become _____ rocks.

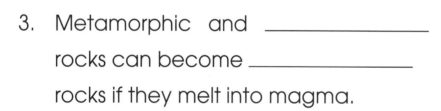

3. Metamorphic and _____ rocks can become _____ rocks if they melt into magma.

4. How do metamorphic rocks become igneous rocks?

_____

5. How do sedimentary rocks become metamorphic rocks?

_____

ISBN: 978-1-897457-76-4

6. How do igneous rocks become sedimentary rocks?

_____

7. What happens to sedimentary rocks when they are exposed to heat and pressure?

_____

melt into magma

erosion

Sedimentary Rock

heat + pressure

erosion

C. Read the paragraph. Then complete the diagram.

The rock cycle shows us that heat and pressure can turn both sedimentary and igneous rocks into metamorphic rocks. Here are some examples. Sandstone and limestone, common sedimentary rocks, turn into quartzite and marble respectively. Shale, a sedimentary rock made of silt, becomes slate. Granite, a common igneous rock, becomes gneiss.

_____ Rock

| Sedimentary Rock | _____ |
| Igneous Rock | _____ |

heat + pressure

_____

_____

_____

_____

5 How We Use Rocks

Rocks are used in almost every aspect of life: building, art, electricity, and more. They are also important to palaeontology, the study of prehistoric life. In this unit, you will learn about some of the many ways people use rocks.

Taj Mahal

After completing this unit, you will

- know where metals are found.
- understand why rocks are important to people.
- know what fossils are and understand why they are important to palaeontologists.

The Taj Mahal was built 300 years ago. You can see that this structure is strong and stable because it was built with marble.

Vocabulary

palaeontology: the study of prehistoric life

metal: a class of minerals with special characteristics

ammonite: fossilized shell of an extinct sea animal

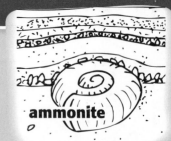

ammonite

ISBN: 978-1-897457-76-4

Have you noticed that many things around you are made from rocks? The concrete foundation of your house, the glass of your windows, the tiles in your bathroom, and even the metal pipes moving heat and water through your house are made from rocks. Metals are found in rocks, and they are one of the most important materials we get from the earth. Check and list things in your house that are made from rocks or metals.

A. Fill in the blanks with the given words. Then circle the metals.

ore   quarries   minerals

Metals are 1._____ found in rocks. When they are extracted from rock, the rock is called 2._____ . Metals, other minerals, and rocks are extracted from sites called mines or 3._____ .

a copper key

Metals

lead	salt	silver	nickel
gold	shale	sand	tin
iron	water	aluminum	oxygen

B. **Write the correct heading to show the area of life in which rock is used. Then complete the descriptions with the given words.**

jewellery energy art construction transportation

trains concrete coal diamonds colour
oil steel sculptures

1. _____

- Marble is a rock used for _____ .

- The pigments that give paint _____ come from minerals.

2. _____

- Cars, airplanes, ships, and _____ are made of _____ and aluminum, which are metals.

3. _____

- Steel from iron and _____ from various rocks are important building materials.

4. _____

- _____ , a rock made from organic matter, is used for electricity and heat.

- Fossils, the things from which _____ is made, are held in rocks.

5. _____

- Gold, silver, and _____ make beautiful things.

ISBN: 978-1-897457-76-4

C. Read the paragraph. Answer the questions. Then put the pictures in order from 1 to 4.

Palaeontology is the study of prehistoric life. Palaeontologists are able to study prehistoric life because of rocks. Rocks hold fossils, which are traces of things that lived long ago. Only sedimentary rocks provide the ideal conditions for fossils, as sediment slowly covers once-living organisms, mineralizes them, and turns into rock around them. Most fossils are never found, but erosion and human activity expose some, allowing palaeontologists to do their work.

1. Why are rocks important to palaeontologists?

    _____

    _____

2. What kinds of rocks hold fossils?

    _____

3.

Ammonite Fossil Formation

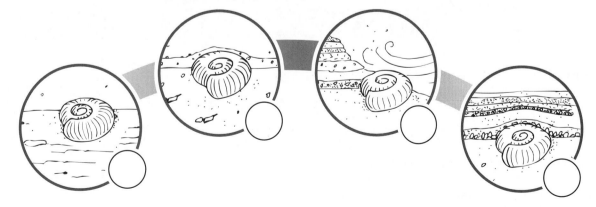

6 More about How We Use Rocks

The use of rocks is important to people, but the outcomes of this use can be both positive and negative. In this unit, you will see that the use of rocks affects people and the environment.

After completing this unit, you will

- understand that people's use of rocks has both positive and negative effects.

- understand that recycling helps preserve limited resources.

bricks from old, crumbling houses

Vocabulary

recycle: treat or process something to make it suitable for reuse

resource: something that can be drawn upon

raw material: a material found in nature

manufacture: make a product from raw materials

one way to recycle

ISBN: 978-1-897457-76-4

Rocks are not just important parts of everyday products; they provide jobs for many people. Some people sell brick, concrete, patio stones, and much more. Carpenters build houses with rock. Miners extract minerals and rock from the earth. Factory workers make steel for cars and car parts, cans for food and drinks, and much more, from rock. Interview your parents or neighbours to see if they work with rocks in some way.

I am a landscaper. I use plants and rocks to design gardens.

A. Check the correct circles.

Impact that Quarries and Mines Have on Communities and Ecosystems:

☺ **Positive**

- Ⓐ create jobs
- Ⓑ create habitats
- Ⓒ cause damage to cars
- Ⓓ quarried stone is used to make concrete for buildings
- Ⓔ supply factories with raw materials
- Ⓕ can be used as swimming pools

☹ **Negative**

- Ⓐ cause air and water pollution
- Ⓑ destroy habitats
- Ⓒ attract mice and other rodents
- Ⓓ remove rich topsoil from the earth
- Ⓔ disturb wildlife
- Ⓕ support invasive species

B. Read the scenario. Decide whether each person is affected positively or negatively and explain your idea. Then write an example of one more person in the community who is affected and write how.

A mine has opened outside Big Rock. It provides people with jobs and the factory with raw materials to manufacture steel for cars. However, it disturbs the local habitat, and the residents of the Aboriginal community close by worry about how it will affect their drinking water.

MINE - OUTSIDE
BIG ROCK

1. **Factory Owner**: _____ affected

   _____

   _____

2. **Resident of the Aboriginal Community**: _____ affected

   _____

   _____

3. **Miner**: _____ affected

   _____

   _____

4. _____ : _____ affected

   _____

   _____

   ISBN: 978-1-897457-76-4

C. Fill in the blanks to complete the paragraph. Then answer the questions.

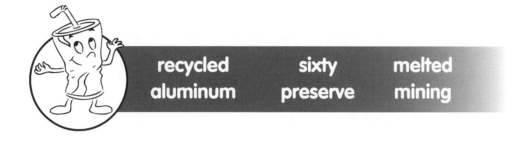

recycled   sixty   melted

aluminum   preserve   mining

Do you drink pop or juice from cans? Do you put your empty cans in the recycling bin? You should, because the 1._____ that cans are made from is one of the most recyclable materials on Earth. An empty can is 2._____ down, re-moulded, re-filled, and back on grocery store shelves in as little as 3._____ days. Also, aluminum can be 4._____ again and again. Recycling aluminum is less expensive than 5._____ it; and not having to mine new aluminum helps us 6._____ our resources.

7. In what ways is recycling aluminum better than mining it?

   _____

   _____

8. Apart from aluminum, what goes in the recycling bin that is made from rocks or minerals?

   _____

 **Experiment**

Introduction

Glaciers and moving water erode rocks, but what about the seasonal freezing and thawing of water in the ground that takes place every year? Does this seasonal freezing and thawing erode rocks, too?

 **Hypothesis**

Seasonal freezing and thawing erodes rocks.

Steps

1. Place all of your rock samples in the plastic container.

2. Pour enough water into the container to cover the rock samples.

3. Put the lid on the container.

4. Place the container in the freezer.

The rock samples can be bought from a gardening store.

Materials

- *5 to 10 different rock samples*
- *a plastic container with a lid (e.g. an empty margarine container)*
- *water*

ISBN: 978-1-897457-76-4

5. Once the water is frozen, take the container out of the freezer and let the ice melt somewhere warm, for example, by a sunny window. Repeat this about 10 times.

6. Once the water has melted for the final time, carefully take the rock samples out of the container without spilling the water.

7. Record. (What, if anything, was left in the water?)

_____

Result

Did the freezing and melting break apart, or erode, the rock samples?

_____

Conclusion

The hypothesis was: _____

_____

My experiment _____ the
hypothesis.   supported / did not support

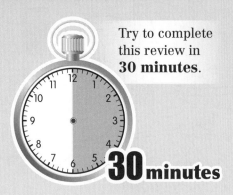

Try to complete this review in **30 minutes**.

30 minutes

This review consists of five sections, from A to E. The marks for each question are shown in parentheses. The circle at the bottom right corner is for the marks you get in each section. An overall record is on the last page of the review.

A. Write T for true and F for false.

1. Erosion is an important factor in the formation of igneous rocks. **(2)** _____

2. Palaeontology is the study of the earth. **(2)** _____

3.    Metamorphic rocks often have fossils. **(2)**

_____

4.    Sedimentary rocks often have visible layers. **(2)**

_____

8

ISBN: 978-1-897457-76-4

B. Do the matching.

1.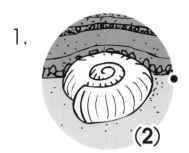
(2)

2.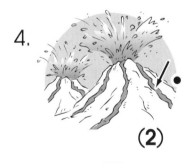
(2)

3.
(2)

4.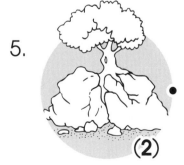
(2)

5.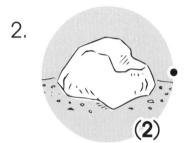
(2)

- the most recycled metal on Earth

- the breaking off, breaking down, and moving of rock

- liquid rock above the earth's surface

- fossilized shell of an extinct sea animal

- solid, inorganic, made up of one or more minerals

C. Read the descriptions and identify the material in each box. Then answer the question.

Materials: **rock   mineral   dung**

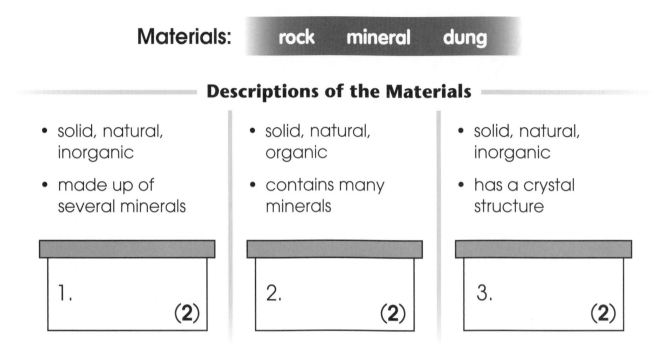

Descriptions of the Materials

- solid, natural, inorganic
- made up of several minerals

1. _____ **(2)**

- solid, natural, organic
- contains many minerals

2. _____ **(2)**

- solid, natural, inorganic
- has a crystal structure

3. _____ **(2)**

4. Name the properties of the mineral that are revealed with the tests. Describe how to carry out the tests. Then circle the described mineral.

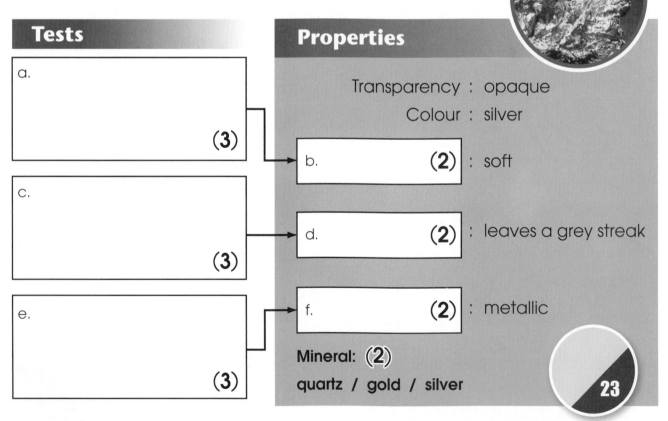

Tests	Properties
a. _____ **(3)**	Transparency : opaque
	Colour : silver
	b. _____ **(2)** : soft
c. _____ **(3)**	d. _____ **(2)** : leaves a grey streak
e. _____ **(3)**	f. _____ **(2)** : metallic
	Mineral: **(2)**
	quartz / gold / silver

23

ISBN: 978-1-897457-76-4

D. Name the types of igneous rocks and circle the words. Then complete the diagram.

1. _____ **(3)** igneous rock

• made from magma
• with **small / large** crystals **(2)**

2. _____ **(3)** igneous rock

• made from lava
• with **small / large** crystals **(2)**

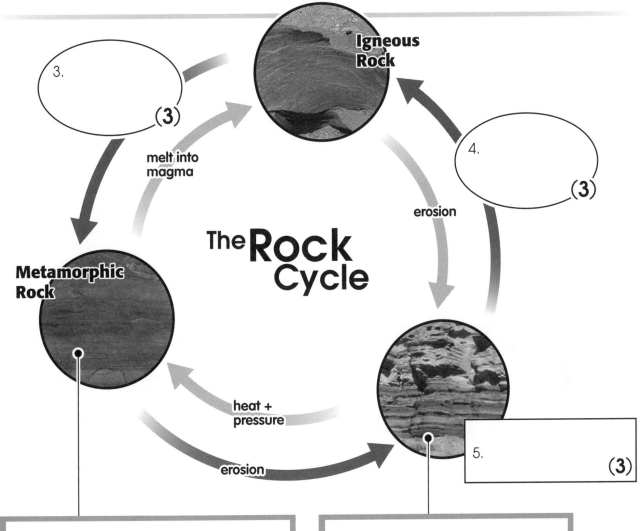

3. _____ **(3)**

melt into magma

Igneous Rock

4. _____ **(3)**

erosion

The **Rock Cycle**

Metamorphic Rock

heat + pressure

erosion

5. _____ **(3)**

made from:

6. _____ **(3)**

• contains **a lot of / no** fossils **(2)**

made from:

7. _____ **(3)**

• **may / never** have fossils **(2)**

29

ISBN: 978-1-897457-76-4

E. Answer the questions.

1. How are these people affected by a new mine in the community?

   An Ecologist   A Factory Worker

   a. a factory worker (**5**)

   _____

   _____

   b. an ecologist (**5**)

   _____

   _____

   affected positively or negatively?

2. Name two places where we can find rocks. (**4**)

   _____

3. What is magma? (**4**)

   _____

4. Describe how rock is important to these areas of life:

   a. energy (**3**)

   _____

   b. construction (**3**)

   _____

5. Write two advantages recycling or reusing rocks and minerals has over mining new ones. (**6**)

   • _____

   • _____

   30

ISBN: 978-1-897457-76-4

My Record

Section A	8
Section B	10
Section C	23
Section D	29
Section E	30

Total

100

80-100

Great work! You really understand your science stuff! Research your favourite science topics at the library or on the Internet to find out more about the topics related to this section. Keep challenging yourself to learn more!

60-79

Good work! You understand some basic concepts, but try reading through the units again to see whether you can master the material! Go over the questions that you had trouble with to make sure you know the correct answers.

below 60

You can do much better! Try reading over the units again. Ask your parents or teachers any questions you might have. Once you feel confident that you know the material, try the review again. Science is exciting, so don't give up!

The Geologist-Astronaut

Harrison Schmitt is a geologist with an impressive work history: he has been to the moon to collect lunar rock samples!

Harrison Schmitt was born on July 3, 1935 in New Mexico, the United States. He received his PhD in geology, and worked as a geologist in Norway and Arizona, the United States. In 1965, he was hired by the National Aeronautics and Space Administration (NASA). There, he continued to work as a geologist and trained to be an astronaut. He examined and evaluated lunar samples collected by astronauts during their space missions. In December 1972, he travelled to the moon as a crew member of the Apollo 17, which was the final NASA mission to the moon. During his mission, he logged almost 302 hours in space with 22 hours spent on the moon's surface to collect samples. Schmitt and the rest of the Apollo 17 crew brought 115 kilograms worth of lunar material back to Earth. Today, Schmitt is retired and lives in New Mexico.

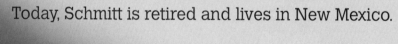

ISBN: 978-1-897457-76-4

Cool Science Facts

1 Can rocks float?

2 Which minerals does the human body need to stay healthy?

3 What is the most common rock on Earth?

4 What kinds of rocks and minerals can you find on the moon? Are they the same as the ones on Earth?

5 Of these three types of rock, which is the oldest?

igneous rock   *sedimentary rock*   *metamorphic rock*

Find the answers on the next page.

ISBN: 978-1-897457-76-4

Cool Science Facts

2 Our bodies need certain minerals in order to be healthy. Calcium, zinc, and iron are some of them. We get these minerals from food, like milk, meat, and eggs.

white wheat bread (rich in zinc)
• for keeping the skin healthy

ham (rich in iron)
• for healthy brain development

milk (rich in protein)
• for building bones and teeth

pumice

1 Most rocks cannot float but one rock called pumice can. It is light enough to float because it has tiny gas pockets formed in a violent volcanic eruption, followed by rapid cooling.

ISBN: 978-1-897457-76-4

4 The most prevalent rocks (basalt) and minerals (feldspar) on the moon are the same as the ones on Earth. Just like on Earth, these lunar rocks originated from volcanoes.

feldspar

basalt

3 The most common rock on Earth is basalt, which is an extrusive volcanic rock. Since it is very durable, we use it in roads and flooring tiles. Ancient Egyptians also used basalt to make statues and the pavements in necropolises, which are ancient cemeteries.

Egyptian basalt statue

5 Igneous rock is the oldest. Sedimentary and metamorphic rocks formed from pre-existing rocks.

THE OLDEST

ISBN: 978-1-897457-76-4

ISBN: 978-1-897457-76-4

Answers

ISBN: 978-1-897457-76-4

Answers

1 Biomes

A. Check: in gardens ; in forests
   Circle: dark ; warm ; wet
   Check: leaves ; fruits

B. 1. grasses
   2. elephants
   3. hot
   4. camels
   5. water
   6. treeless
   7. coldest
   8. precipitation
   9. permafrost
   10. cushion plants
   11. life
   12. ferns
   13. insects
   14. plankton
   15. blue whale

C. Tropical
   Location: equator
   Precipitation: 150 cm
   Temperature: warm
   Animal: giant anteater, anaconda, jaguar
   Plant: broadleaf trees
   Temperate
   Location: equator ; west
   Precipation: 300 cm each year
   Temperature: cool
   Animal: black bear, cougar, salmon, bald eagle
   Plant: giant coniferous trees

2 Habitats and Communities

A.

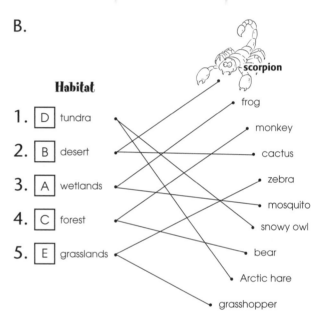

B.

C. (Suggested features)
   1. webbed feet to swim ; feathers that are waterproof
   2. hard, pointed beak to crack seeds ; flexible claws to hold onto branches
   3. thick stem to store water ; small leaves to minimize water loss
   4. thick, furry coat ; white fur to blend into the snow
   5. strong, fast runner ; stripes act as a camouflage from predators

D. 1. B

  2. A

  3. A ; C

  4. The panda's habitat is being destroyed, so there is a huge decrease in the amount of bamboo and land space.

3 Changes to Habitats

A. Check: A, C, E

B. 1. human ; deforestation

  2. natural ; wildfire

  3. human ; farming

  4. human ; oil spill

  5. natural ; flooding

C. 1. B

  2. A

  3. F

  4. C

  5. D

  6. E

D. 1. (Individual pictures)

  Canadian Arctic:

  snow, ice, and frozen ground

  the rise of temperature

  Sea ice melts earlier each spring.

  Polar Bear:

  A thick layer of fat keeps them warm.

  Huge, rough paws give them traction on the ice.

  Polar bears have fewer days to hunt, so they have less food.

  Their thick layer of fat shrinks, so they cannot keep warm.

2. (Suggested answer)

  Polar Bears International works to protect polar bears by funding research that educates people on the conditions of polar bears and their habitat.

Experiment

(Individual experiment outcome)

4 Our Interaction with Habitats

A. (Suggested examples)

  1. jewellery

  2. cooking foil

  3. drinks

  4. jewellery

  5. electricity

  6. cooking

  7. coal ; producing heat

B. 1. A   2. C

  3. B   4. A

  5. A ; C

  (Individual idea)

C. 1. (Individual picture)

  2. It is located in Alberta's Rocky Mountains.

  3. Mountainous terrain, glaciers and ice fields, coniferous forests, and alpine meadows can be found there.

  4. (Suggested answer)

  Banff National Park is home to grizzly bears, cougars, pine trees, and fir trees.

5. (Suggested answer)
Park workers monitor species to see how human activities affect the population. They also set controlled fires to encourage new plant growth.

5 Food Chains

A. 1. A
   2. B
   3. C, D
B. 1. producers
   2. consumers
   3. decomposers
   4. Producers
   5. Consumers
   6. Decomposers

Food Chain

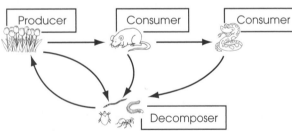

C. A: consumer
   B: producer
   C: producer
   D: decomposer
   E: consumer
D. (Suggested answers)
   1. cow
   2. grass ; fox
   3. mouse
   4. algae ➡ shrimp ➡ Arctic cod ➡ seal ➡ polar bear

E. 1a. important
   b. enzymes
   c. decomposers
   d. waste
   2. Decomposers include bacteria, fungi, and worms.
   3. Decomposers break down dead plant and animal matter into essential nutrients which producers need to make food.
   4. Check: A, B, E, F

6 What Animals Eat

A. 1. Check: C, D, E
   2. They have sharp teeth.
   3. They eat plants.
B. 1. Producers
   2. consumers
   3. herbivores
   4. carnivores
   5. omnivores
   6. Herbivores
   7. A: herbivore
      B: omnivore
      C: carnivore
      D: omnivore
      E: carnivore
C. 1. caterpillar ; bird (omnivore) ; bobcat (carnivore)
   2. grasshopper (herbivore) ; lizard (omnivore) ; snake (carnivore)
   3. The rest of the organisms in the food chain would die.

4. Without the lizard eating the grasshoppers, grasshoppers would become overpopulated. This means there would not be enough grass for the grasshopper to eat, and many grasshoppers would then die. Snakes may also die out because their food source is gone.

D. 1a. F

   b. T

   c. F

   d. T

2. A blue whale's favourite food is krill. It eats up to 40 million krill per day.

3. plankton ; krill ; blue whale

4. Krill would not be able to survive, and without krill, blue whales would not survive either.

Experiment

(Individual experiment outcome)

Review

A. 1. T

   2. F

   3. F

   4. T

B.
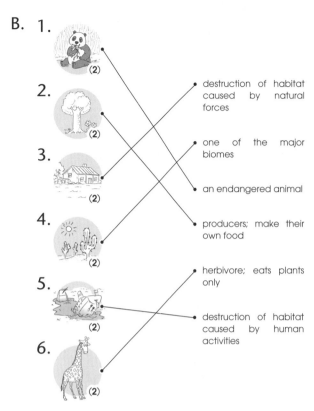

1.
2.
3.
4.
5.
6.

- destruction of habitat caused by natural forces
- one of the major biomes
- an endangered animal
- producers; make their own food
- herbivore; eats plants only
- destruction of habitat caused by human activities

C. 1. grasslands

It has a long neck that helps it reach high into trees to obtain leaves.

2. wetlands

It has webbed feet that help it swim.

D. (Suggested answers)

1. building houses and deforestation

2. wildfire and flooding

3. The animals' habitat will be destroyed. The logging activity will create job opportunities for the community.

E. (Suggested examples)

1. a plant that makes its own food using energy from the sun

example: tree

2. an organism that feeds on plants or other animals

example: human

3. an organism that breaks down the bodies of dead plants and animals
example: earthworm

4.

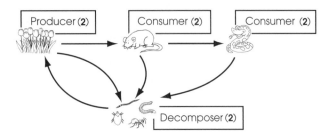

F. 1. tundra

lichen ➡ lemming ➡ snowy owl ➡ Arctic fox

2. forest

fern ➡ deer ➡ cougar

3. ocean

plankton ➡ fish ➡ seal ➡ white shark

4. Deer and cougars would die out.

5. An arrow means "is eaten by". It represents a transfer of energy and nutrients.

Section 2

1 Machines in the Past

A. 1. inclined

easier

2. wheel ; axle

easier

B. 1. lever   2. fulcrum
3. sling   4. rock
5. rope   6. weight
7a. sling   b. rock
  c. lever   d. rope
  e. fulcrum   f. weight
8a. 3   b. 4
  c. 2   d. 1

C. 1a. lever   b. fulcrum
   c. weight   d. rope

2.

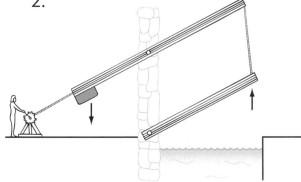

2 Simple Machines

A. Check: A, C, D, F

B. 1. A: unable

B: able

pulleys ; greater ; increased

2. counter-clockwise ; faster speeds ; small ; faster

C. 1. B

Eloise's pushing down on the stick is the effort. The small rock is the fulcrum. The large rock is the load.

2. Check: A, C

3. (Suggested answers)

a. pizza cutter

b. bicycle

ISBN: 978-1-897457-76-4

3 Gears

A. (Make cardboard gears.)

B. 1a. counter-clockwise

  b. clockwise

 2. yes

 3.

Gears	A	B	C
Direction	↘	↗	↘
	↗	↘	↗

 4. counter-clockwise

C. 1. twice

 2. faster

 3. counter-clockwise

 4. It turns twice in a clockwise direction.

 5. Yes, the speeds of both gears are the same and they move in the same direction.

D.1a. F   b. T

  c. T   d. T

 2. Biking on Level Ground:
   front (50 teeth) and rear (15 teeth)
   move fast
   hard to pedal
   Biking Uphill:
   front (20 teeth) and rear (40 teeth)
   move slowly
   easy to pedal

Experiment

(Possible experiment outcome)

 5. faster than
   the same as

Result:

 Yes, they did.

Conclusion:

 The speeds of rotation of gears of the same size are the same even if there is another gear between them.; supported

4 Gears around Us

A. 1. lever
   wheel and axle

 2. screw
   lever
   wheel and axle

B. 1. spur gears ; shafts ; one

 2. bevel gears ; direction ; two

 3. worm gear ; worm ; two

 4. idler gear ; same ; one

C. 1.

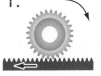   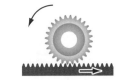

The rack moves to the left.   The rack moves to the right.

 2. linear

 3. Check: B, C, D

ISBN: 978-1-897457-76-4

D.1a. no b. yes
  2. (Suggested answers)
     Way 1: She can add a third gear between the dolls.

     Way 2: She can move them apart and link them with a chain.

  3. She can use two gears of different sizes.

5 Pulleys Everywhere

A. Check: A, C, F
B. (Trace the arrows.)
  1a. wheel b. rope
   c. effort d. load
  2. up
C.1a. 50 N b. 50 N
  2a. 80 N b. 80 N
  3. the same ; easier
  4. weight

5.

D. 1. in recreation: pulleys – keeps rock climbers safe

   in construction: cranes – move construction materials

   in shipping: forklifts – lift and lower heavy loads

   in building maintenance: hanging scaffolding – lifts and lowers workers

   at home: pulleys – lift and lower garage doors

   in restaurants: dumbwaiters – move food between floors
  2a. downward b. upwards

6 Pulley Power

A. A fixed pulley at the top of the flagpole means that when you pull down on one end of the rope, the flag on the other end is raised. Your pulling is the effort.
B. 1a. 200 N
   b. 100 N
  2a. 420 N
   b. 210 N
  3. half
  4. The effort needed decreases.

C. 1. Experiment 1: 100 N ; 10 cm
     Experiment 2: 50 N ; 20 cm
 2. half ; doubled
 3. The distance increases.

D. 1. A
 2.

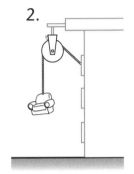

3a. 1000 N   b. 500 N

Experiment

(Possible experiment outcome)
Result: A
Conclusion:

It is easier to lift things with a movable pulley than with just your arm. ; supported

Review

A. 1. T
  2. T
  3. F
  4. T

B.

1. 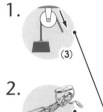 (3)
2. (3)
3. (3)
4. (3)
5. (3)

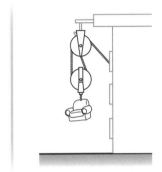

an idler gear; keeps the two connected gears rotating in the same direction

a rack and pinion system; a single gear meshing with a sliding toothed rack

a compound machine with a lever, gears, and a wheel and axle

a combination of a circular gear and a worm gear

a pulley; the load goes up when the free end of the rope is pulled down

C. 1. It is a pulley attached to a fixed structure above the load being lifted.
 2. It is a pulley attached to the load being lifted.
 3. (Suggested answers)
   Tie back long hair and make sure pulleys and gears are fastened securely before testing them with a load.
 4. 40 N more effort is needed to lift the load.
 5. Gear A will turn clockwise. Gears B and D will turn counter-clockwise.

D. 1.

2. C   3. C

E. 1. (Suggested diagrams)

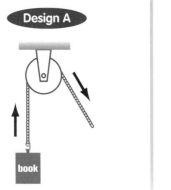

2a. 20

b. 10

3. Design A cannot reduce the force needed, but it is still easier because it allows us to use our weight to lift a load.

Section 3

1 Light around Us

A. (Suggested examples)
natural ; A ; sun
artificial ; B ; flashlight

B. 1. emit
2. reflect
3. emit
4. A, D, H
5. B, C, E, F, G
6. C and E are safety reflectors. They keep people safe by reflecting car lights at night so that drivers can see them.

C. 1. straight
2. direction
3. reflected
4. Check: A

5. Check: B
6. Check: A

2 Light: Reflection and Refraction

A.

Properties of Light

When light hits an object and bounces off, it creates a __reflection__ .

Light travels in a straight line, but when it passes through another medium such as water, it may bend and change direction. This is called __refraction__ .

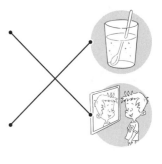

B. 1. white
2. red
3. orange
4. yellow
5. green
6. blue
7. indigo
8. violet
9. raindrop
10. direction
11. refraction
(Colour as indicated.)

C. A: white ; reflects
B: black ; absorbed
C: yellow ; absorbed
When light hits a green frog, its skin absorbs every colour but green.

3 Light: Transparency

A. (Colour as indicated.)
1. transparent
2. translucent
3. opaque

B.

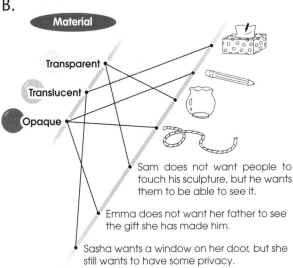

Sam does not want people to touch his sculpture, but he wants them to be able to see it.

Emma does not want her father to see the gift she has made him.

Sasha wants a window on her door, but she still wants to have some privacy.

C. (Suggested answers)

transparent: The windshield of a car should be transparent.

translucent: Curtains can be translucent so that light can pass through them, but at the same time, they can give you privacy.

opaque: Change rooms for a clothing store should be opaque.

D. 1. straight
2. shadow
3. opaque
4. length
5. ✗
6. ✔
7. ✔

4 What Is Sound?

A. 1. vibrates
2. vibrate
3. vibrating
4. sound

B. Experiment 1:
yes ; can
Experiment 2:
yes ; Sound can travel through water.
Experiment 3:
yes ; Sound can travel through solids.

C. 1. low
2. (Individual example)
3. fast ; high
4. (Individual example)

5 What Happens to Sound

A. 1. loudness
2. decibels
3. a jackhammer
4. a busy street
5. a whisper

B. 1. reflected ; hard
richer
An echo
2. absorbed ; soft
Carpeting
absorbing
3. modified
Loudness ; louder
Pitch ; higher

Experiment

(Individual experiment outcome)

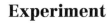

C. outer
earflap ; ear canal
eardrum
middle
tiny bones
inner
cochlea
nerves

4. communicate
5. echo
6. surface
7. air
8. water

Experiment
(Individual experiment outcome)

6 How We Use Light and Sound

A.

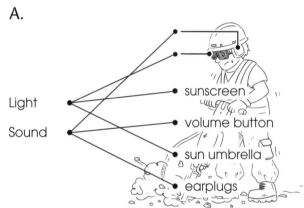

(Suggested answer)
Too much light can damage our eyes and too much sound can damage our ears.

B. 1. A ; light
2. E ; light
3. D ; light
4. B ; sound
5. C ; sound
   F ; sound

C. 1. sound
2. whale
3. echolocation

Review

A. 1. T
2. T
3. F
4. F

B.

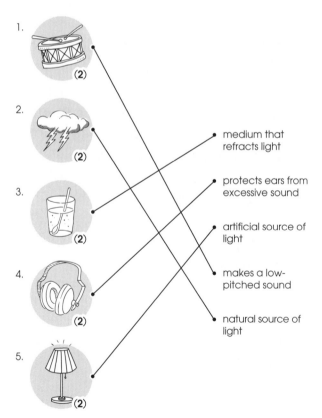

   ISBN: 978-1-897457-76-4

C. 1. Check: A, C, D, F
   Cross out: B, E
 2a. Light can be absorbed.
  b. Light can be refracted.
 3. When light hits the apple, it absorbs all the colours in the light except red, which is reflected.

D. 1. Check: B, C, D, F
   Cross out: A, E
 2. Check: A
   Sound reflects off smooth and hard surfaces, but not soft and rough surfaces.
 3a. The vibrating band makes the air around it vibrate.
  b. The sound will be louder because the vibrations will be bigger.

E. 1. A: eardrum ;
      vibrates with sound waves
   B: cochlea ;
      changes vibrations into signals
   C: nerves ;
      carry the signals to the brain
 2a. (Suggested answer)
   sunglasses
  b. (Suggested answer)
   earplugs
  c. hearing aid
  d. telescope

Section 4

1 Rocks and Minerals
A. Check: A, D, E, F, G, H, J, K, L
   (Individual example)

B. 1. Type: mineral
   inorganic ; crystal ; diamond
   Type: rock
   natural ; minerals ; sandstone
 2. They are both solid, natural, and inorganic.
 3. Minerals are made up of one thing; rocks are often made up of more than one thing.
 4. rock ; mineral ; rock

C. 1. the study of the earth
 2. rocks and minerals
 3. land movement long ago
 4. what is at the Earth's centre
 5. where earthquakes are likely to occur
 6. when volcanoes are likely to erupt

2 Minerals
A. 1. transparency ; translucent
 2. lustre ; dull
 3. colour
 4. hardness ; soft
 5. streak

B. 1. hardness
 2. streak
 3. lustre, transparency, colour
 4. turquoise ; waxy ; opaque
 5. gold ; metallic ; opaque
 6. quartz ; glassy ; translucent

C. Talc ; 3 ; 4 ; 6 ; Quartz ; 9 ; Diamond
 1. diamond
 2. gypsum ; talc
 3. (Suggested answer)
   orthoclase and apatite

Answers

3 Rocks

A.

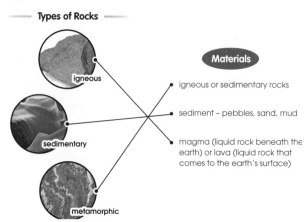

Types of Rocks

Materials

igneous → magma (liquid rock beneath the earth) or lava (liquid rock that comes to the earth's surface)

sedimentary → igneous or sedimentary rocks

metamorphic → sediment – pebbles, sand, mud

B. 1. Igneous
   a. magma ; cools ; granite
   b. lava ; small ; obsidian
   2. Sedimentary
      layers ; under ; fossils ; sandstone
   3. Metamorphic
      extreme ; rarely ; gneiss ; marble

Experiment

(Possible experiment outcome)

Result:

Some of the rocks reacted with the vinegar.

Conclusion:

Some rocks react with vinegar – an acid like acid rain – and some do not. ; supported

4 The Rock Cycle

A. 1. sand
   2. mountains
   3. moving water
   4. erosion
   5. sedimentary
   6. cycle

B. 1. sedimentary ; metamorphic
   2. igneous ; erosion ; sedimentary
   3. sedimentary ; igneous
   4. They melt into magma.
   5. They are under intense heat and pressure.
   6. They erode.
   7. They become metamorphic rocks.

C.

Sedimentary Rock		Metamorphic Rock
sandstone		quartzite
limestone	heat + pressure	marble
shale		slate
Igneous Rock granite		gneiss

5 How We Use Rocks

A. 1. minerals
   2. ore
   3. quarries
   lead ; silver ; nickel ; gold ; tin ; iron ; aluminum

B. 1. art ; sculptures ; colour
   2. transportation ; trains ; steel
   3. construction ; concrete
   4. energy ; Coal ; oil
   5. jewellery ; diamonds

C. 1. Rocks are important because they hold fossils, which palaeontologists study.
   2. sedimentary rocks
   3. 1 ; 2 ; 4 ; 3

6   More about How We Use Rocks

A.   Positive

Check: A, D, E

Negative

Check: A, B, D, E

B.   (Suggested answers)

1.   positively ; The factory owner will have raw materials to supply his factory close at hand.

2.   negatively ; The resident is worried about how his or her water supply will be affected.

3.   positively ; If he or she is out of a job, the miner will surely get one now.

4.   Ecologist ; negatively ; The ecologist is worried about how the mine will affect the local habitat.

C.   1.   aluminum

2.   melted

3.   sixty

4.   recycled

5.   mining

6.   preserve

7.   It is less expensive and it preserves resources.

8.   Glass is made from rock, and it can be recycled.

Experiment

(Possible experiment outcome)

7.   Small pieces of rock were left in the water.

Result:

Yes, it did.

Conclusion: Seasonal freezing and thawing erodes rocks. ; supported

Review

A.   1.   F

2.   F

3.   F

4.   T

B.

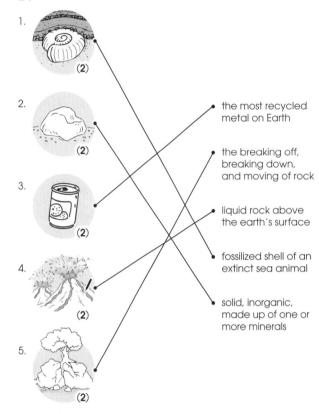

1.   fossilized shell of an extinct sea animal

2.   solid, inorganic, made up of one or more minerals

3.   the most recycled metal on Earth

4.   liquid rock above the earth's surface

5.   the breaking off, breaking down, and moving of rock

C.   1.   rock

2.   dung

3.   mineral

4a.   Scratch the mineral with another mineral.

b.   Hardness

c.   Rub the mineral on a rough surface to see if it leaves a streak.

d.   Streak

e.   Observe how light interacts with the mineral.

f.   Lustre

Mineral: silver

D. 1. intrusive ; large
   2. extrusive ; small
   3. heat + pressure
   4. melt into magma
   5. Sedimentary Rock
   6. igneous and sedimentary rocks ;
      no
   7. igneous and metamorphic rocks ;
      may

E. (Suggested answers)
   1a. A factory worker would be affected
       positively because she would have
       a supply of raw material to work
       with.
    b. An ecologist would be affected
       negatively because he would be
       worried about the mine's impact
       on the ecosystem.
    2. (Any two of the following)
       mountain, sea floor, beach, garden
       soil, desert, cave, underground,
       volcano, forest floor
    3. Magma is liquid rock below the
       Earth's surface.
   4a. Oil comes from fossils, which are
       held in rocks. Coal, used for heat
       and electricity, is a rock.
    b. Steel and concrete, which are
       made from rocks, are important
       building materials.
    5. costs less than mining new ones ;
       preserves resources

TRIVIA

Questions

ISBN: 978-1-897457-76-4

ISBN: 978-1-897457-76-4

Can flying squirrels actually fly?

All deserts are hot.

All the shining dots we see in the night sky are stars.

Which of the following is not a source of natural light?

A. the sun
B. a lamp
C. a firefly
D. stars

Answer:

No, they cannot.

They float like parachutes, but they cannot fly like birds.

Answer:

false

Some of them are planets, like Venus and Jupiter, and others are artificial satellites.

Answer:

false

Antarctica is one of the largest cold deserts because its annual precipitation is very low.

Answer:

B. a lamp

ISBN: 978-1-897457-76-4

True or False?

A diamond never melts.

How long does it take for moonlight to reach the Earth?

A. 1.25 seconds

B. 1.25 hours

C. 1.25 days

Where would you find a cricket's ears?

A. on its head

B. on its chest

C. on its front legs

D. crickets don't have ears

What is the diameter of the largest snowflake recorded?

A. 0.5 mm

B. 2 m

C. 38 cm

ISBN: 978-1-897457-76-4

Answer:

false

All minerals melt if the temperature is high enough. Diamonds melt at 3547°C.

Answer:

A. 1.25 seconds

Answer:

C. on its front legs

Answer:

C. 38 cm

A huge snowflake landed in Montana, U.S. in 1887.

ISBN: 978-1-897457-76-4

Which flying mammal uses sound to "see"?

A. a butterfly

B. a bat

C. a snake

True or False

A strand of spider silk that goes around the Earth would weigh less than 500 g (a weight of 3 apples).

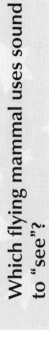

Where is the windiest place on Earth?

A. in Antarctica

B. in Japan

C. in Ontario

WARNING
STRONG WIND

Which of the following does the exterior design of the Beijing National Stadium for the 2008 Olympics resemble?

A. a house

B. a bird's nest

C. a beehive

ISBN: 978-1-897457-76-4

Answer:

B. a bat

A bat makes sounds and listens to the echoes that return to it to determine where objects are.

Answer:

true

Spider silk is extremely lightweight.

Answer:

A. in Antarctica

At George V in Antarctica, winds reaching 320 km/h are usual.

Answer:

B. a bird's nest

ISBN: 978-1-897457-76-4

True or False

All adult elephants have tusks.

In a pride of lions, who does more hunting, the females or the males?

If you clang each glass with a spoon, which one will give you the highest pitch?

A.

B.

C.

What is the fastest thing in the universe?

A. a space shuttle

B. light

C. a sports car

ISBN: 978-1-897457-76-4

Answer:

false

Female Asian elephants do not have tusks.

Answer:

A.

Answer:

the female lions

The males' main job is to protect the pride and their territory.

Answer:

B. light

The speed of light is about 300 000 km per second.

ISBN: 978-1-897457-76-4

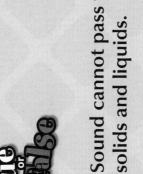

True or False

Some planets emit light and some reflect light.

True or False

Sound cannot pass through solids and liquids.

The Eiffel Tower is taller in summer than in winter. How much taller does it get?

A. 2 cm   B. 15 cm

C. 10 cm   D. 1.2 km

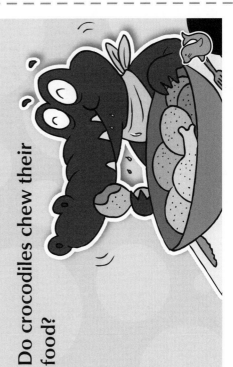

Do crocodiles chew their food?

ISBN: 978-1-897457-76-4

Answer:

false

No planets emit light. They only reflect light. Only stars, like the sun, emit light.

Answer:

B. 15 cm

Heat expands and cool contracts the materials of the tower.

Answer:

false

Sound can travel through solids and liquids where there is air.

Answer:

No, they do not.

Even with all those teeth, crocodiles swallow their food whole.

ISBN: 978-1-897457-76-4

Has the water flow in Niagara Falls ever stopped before?

True or False

Sharks do not have a single bone in their bodies.

Which of these animals has bones?

A. octopus
B. manta ray
C. lobster
D. salmon

About how many giraffes standing on top of each other have the same height as the CN Tower?

A. 10
B. 110
C. 1110

ISBN: 978-1-897457-76-4

Answer:

Yes, it has.

In March of 1848, Niagara Falls dried up for 30 hours because large sheets of ice temporarily blocked the water channel.

Answer:

true

A shark's skeleton is made of cartilage, which is the same material that your nose and ears are made of.

Answer:

D. salmon

Octopi and lobsters are invertebrates. Manta rays are considered vertebrates, but their skeletons are made of cartilage, not bones.

Answer:

B. 110

The CN Tower is 553.3 metres tall and had held the tallest free-standing structure record for 31 years.

ISBN: 978-1-897457-76-4

How old is the Earth?

A. around 2010 years old
B. around 5000 years old
C. around 4.8 billion years old

Which animal did people first domesticate?

A. dog   B. cat
C. cow   D. pig

Do birds have teeth?

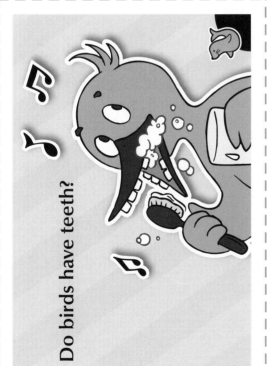

Which of the following animals have not been sent to space?

A. tigers   B. dogs
C. monkeys   D. rats

ISBN: 978-1-897457-76-4

Answer:

C. around 4.8 billion years old

Answer:

No, they do not.

Answer:

D. pig

The Chinese domesticated pigs 7000 years ago.

Answer:

A. tigers

ISBN: 978-1-897457-76-4

There are Northern lights. Are there Southern lights?

True or False

Anything that can pass through a funnel is a liquid.

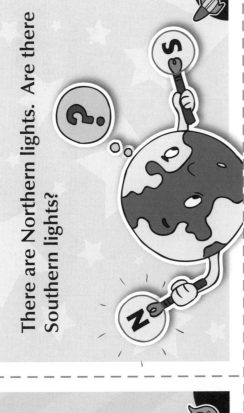

Which animal has wide, flat teeth for munching on grass?

A. lion   B. horse
C. goose   D. snake

True or False

The height of the Great Pyramid of Giza has decreased 7 metres over the last 4500 years.

ISBN: 978-1-897457-76-4

Answer:

Yes, there are.

Southern lights can be viewed near the South Pole.

Answer:

B. horse

Answer:

false

Salt can pass through a funnel, but salt is a solid.

Answer:

true

It is believed that the pyramid has been eroded by natural occurrences.

ISBN: 978-1-897457-76-4

Which part of our bodies is made of the same material as a toucan's beak?

A. nails
B. teeth
C. bones
D. hair

Why is the water in a hot spring hot?

A. Heat from inside the Earth heats up the water.
B. Water is boiled and get poured into the spring.
C. The sun heats up the water in the spring.

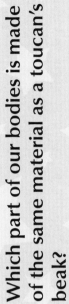

True or False

Mars appears to be reddish because it is a very hot planet.

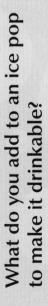

What do you add to an ice pop to make it drinkable?

Answer:

A. nails

A toucan's beak is made of keratin, the same substance that our nails are made of. It is strong but light, which is good, because a toucan's beak is huge!

Answer:

false

Mars appears to be reddish because of the iron oxide in its soil.

Answer:

A. Heat from inside the Earth heats up the water.

Groundwater heated by the Earth's interior reaches the Earth's surface to form hot springs.

Answer:

heat

ISBN: 978-1-897457-76-4

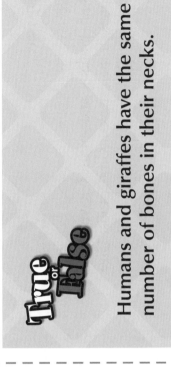

True or False

Like humans, fire needs oxygen.

Humans and giraffes have the same number of bones in their necks.

Which of the following bears is not an omnivore?

A. panda bear   B. grizzly bear
C. polar bear   D. black bear

How many bacteria can a cup of soil hold?

A. about 100 000
B. about the number of people in Canada
C. about the number of people on Earth

ISBN: 978-1-897457-76-4   Complete ScienceSmart • Grade 4   227

Answer:

true

Without oxygen, fire will burn out.

Answer:

C. polar bear

Polar bears eat meat only.

Answer:

true

Both humans and giraffes have seven bones in their necks. Giraffes just have really, really big neck bones.

Answer:

C. about the number of people on Earth

A cup of soil can hold billions of bacteria.

ISBN: 978-1-897457-76-4

Which of these animals can change its diet and its behaviour to survive in a wide range of habitats?

A. coyote
B. flamingo
C. dolphin
D. snowshoe hare

All rocks sink in rivers.

True or False

Why do we see lightning before we hear thunder?

A. Our eyes are in front of our ears.
B. Light travels faster, so it will reach us before sound does.
C. We are more sensitive to light than sound.

Which of these natural structures commonly has 6 sides?

A. a spiderweb
B. a snowflake
C. a bird's nest
D. a lily pad

ISBN: 978-1-897457-76-4

Answer:

A. coyote

Answer:

B. Light travels faster, so it will reach us before sound does.

Answer:

false

Pumice, a very light rock formed from volcanic activity, floats. Air is trapped in the many bubbles in the rock so it can float in water.

Answer:

B. a snowflake

ISBN: 978-1-897457-76-4

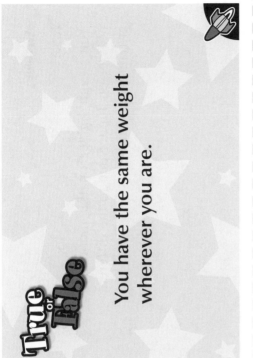

True or False

You have the same weight wherever you are.

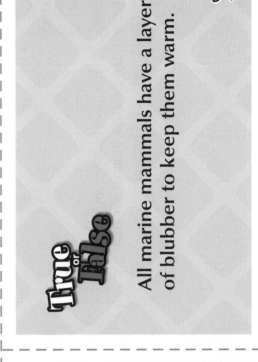

True or False

All marine mammals have a layer of blubber to keep them warm.

Which of the following can be found on the moon?

A. a teddy bear

B. mirrors

C. a cellphone

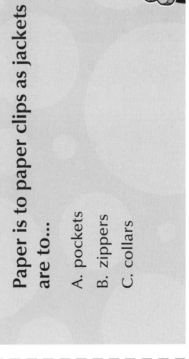

Paper is to paper clips as jackets are to...

A. pockets

B. zippers

C. collars

ISBN: 978-1-897457-76-4

Answer:

false

You weigh lighter on the moon and heavier on Jupiter due to the different gravitational forces.

Answer:

false

Sea otters do not have blubber, but they do have a dense, thick coat of fur that keeps them warm and buoyant.

Answer:

B. mirrors

Mirrors were left on the moon to reflect light so that the distance between the Earth and the moon can be measured.

Answer:

B. zippers

Zippers fasten jackets.

ISBN: 978-1-897457-76-4